Theory of International Physical Education and Sports Studies for the Achievement of Peace

Noriaki Osada

Translated by Andrew Raskin

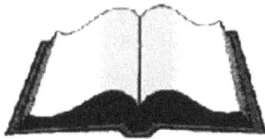

CCB Publishing
British Columbia, Canada

Theory of International Physical Education and Sports Studies
for the Achievement of Peace

Copyright ©2010 by Noriaki Osada
ISBN-13 978-1-926585-67-3
Third Edition

Library and Archives Canada Cataloguing in Publication

Osada, Noriaki, 1949-
Theory of international physical education and sports studies for the achievement of
peace / written by Noriaki Osada; translated by Andrew Raskin – 3rd ed.
Includes bibliographical references.
ISBN 978-1-926585-67-3
1. Physical education and training--Social aspects.
2. Sports--Social aspects. 3. Physical education and training--Research.
4. Sports--Research. 5. International relations. 6. Peace--Social aspects.
I. Raskin, Andrew II. Title.
GV706.5.O83 2009   306.4'83   C2009-907078-2

Cover design: Images utilized are in the public domain and are used without malice.

Publisher: CCB Publishing
             British Columbia, Canada
             www.ccbpublishing.com

To my parents, who passed away before this book was published.

Also to Baron DeCubertin of France, who began the modern Olympic games.

Contents

Preface

I have spent much effort in Japan establishing physical education and sports theory, and I would like to express my thanks to Professor Sasabe of Iwate University for her strong encouragement at the time I was presenting this theory of peace. Furthermore, I would like to acknowledge my meeting with Professor Kenzo Kashiwabara of Graduate Studies at Osaka Education College as the launching of this theory. When I decided to move to the United States to continue my research, I received much support from Professor Shinobu Abe of the Japan Physical Education College, and for this I would like to express my deepest appreciation.

In Japan, I found that my ideas were not being accepted, and on May 18, 1984, I arrived in America, where I hoped I could reach all of the world's physical education and sports scholars. For me, America was a totally unknown world. Relying on a letter from Professor Earl F. Zeigler of Western Ontario University (who was recommended to me by Professor Abe), I went to America and landed at Kennedy Airport. Although five years have passed, I will never forget how I clung to the manuscript of the Ball Game Theory I had written in Japan as if it were a precious jewel. I was longing for the humanistic, beautiful ideals of "freedom" and "democracy" that I hoped to find. As I arrived, I thought to myself that in America I could reach the genius of physical education and sports scholars.

I had to start from scratch in America, but in August, 1987, I received my Green Card, which allows me to be a permanent resident. Presently, I am enjoying a wonderful life in New York City. On September 29,1989, I flew to Western Ontario University in Canada, and the next day I first met Professor Earl F. Zeigler, with whom I had corresponded by mail for quite a long time. This was the first time that I was able to hear from an American his impression of the harmony of the words *Human, Physical Education-Sports, Peace*. For me, this was a very emotional moment. I was able to reconfirm our friendship, which will lead us closer to the realization of world peace. He is a master among the physical education and sports scholars I have met in my life. He is a friend, and is the first American who will strive to establish the World Physical Education and Sports Academy for the realization of world peace. Thank you, Professor Zeigler! With the establishment of physical education and sports studies for the achievement of peace, we will leave our mark in history! Although my progress in America is a result of my own efforts, I would like to express my thanks as an American to the United States government.

In the future, I will go on to complete the *Theory of International Physical Education and Sports Studies for the Achievement of Peace*. In addition, I would like to promote the establishment of an academy that will nurture physical education and sports studies and communicate to all physical education and sports scholars. When this theory is complete and published, I would like to visit the grave of Baron de Cubertin in France and promise that Olympic competition will be for the purpose of peace created by the world's physical education and sports scholars. Today, I can simply pray that the realization of this day will be possible.

Also, I would like to express sincere thanks to Mr. Andrew Raskin, who translated my complex writings from Japanese into English. You are a messenger of world peace, and an American friend whom I will not forget as long as I live. I am very proud of this messenger of peace, a young man who has taken on the burden of the future of America. Thank you America! In the future, through physical education and sports scholarship, we will create a guarantee of peace for the nations of man. Now that I have completed these three theories, I strongly believe that this will come about. Then, we will begin to spread world peace. We will not become a burden to humanity. Instead, we will support humanity in the direction of peace–along with all the world's sports and physical education scholars! This is because we are living in the nations of man.

Introduction

This book was written with three bold intentions: to awaken the physical education and sports scholars of the world to their social, nationalistic, and global responsibilities; to promote the study of physical education and sports as a study of peace independent from other academic fields; and to affirm the value of such study. Until now, physical education and sports studies have been supported by ever-changing governments and by universities. Leadership in the field of physical education and sports studies has come from education doctors, medical doctors, philosophy doctors, and so on. However, education doctors are contributors to education studies, and medical doctors are contributors to medical studies. Thus, it is natural to conclude that physical education and sports studies research carried out within these fields perceive the phenomenon of physical education and sports from the outside. The heart of the phenomenon goes unseen.

I intend to show, in a rigorous theory based on social responsibility, that from now on the physical education and sports scholars of the world must conduct research in physical education and sports studies. Through this book, I hope to provide a method by which the physical education and sports scholars of the world can prosper independently from other institutions (national governments, medical studies, educational studies, universities, etc.). I hope to expose the national and global problems that presently affect physical education and sports scholars. In addition, this exposure will be the beginning of the promotion of physical education and sports studies as a study of peace.

What is the social responsibility of the physical education and sports scholars in each country? It is to guarantee the special human existence that occurs in the practice of all types of ball games, swimming, track and field competition, etc., around the world. This is the overriding national and global responsibility of physical education and sports scholars. In regard to research, physical education, and sports, scholars should not play with words, conduct experiments and surveys without true objectives, or carry out physical education and sports research to fulfill the personal goal of obtaining a doctorate degree from some other academic field. The physical education and sports scholars of the world will, through physical education and sports research, create national theories that will lead to peaceful societies and peaceful nations. We physical education and sports scholars must, through our writings, recognize our social and national responsibility, in order to establish our scholarship as an autonomous academic field. In the future, we must work toward national and global solidarity.

The practice of Olympic competition is the home of the world's physical education and sports scholars. Baron de Coubertin advocated a pure world, using words such as "sportsmanship" and "fair play." This is a world in which one struggles for oneself, for one's country, for the world, and for peace. This world is a unique scholarly world that can be created by no one other than the world's physical education and sports scholars. In order to support the practice of physical education and sports as a practice of peace, the physical education and sports scholars who support this practice must build a world of peace. With our support, the physical education and sports scholars of each nation will form a national theory for the achievement of peace based on physical education and sports research. These theories will be in each country's own language and reflect each country's traditions, history, and thought. It is a natural fact that Soviet physical education and sports scholars have a love for the Soviet nation and its society. Furthermore, it is natural that French physical education and sports scholars have a love for France and its society and that American physical education and sports scholars love the United States and its society. The fact that physical education and sports scholars from different countries have a love for different languages, histories, and traditions reflects the basis of human nations. We must recognize that this condition was inevitable from the birth of nations and individuals. The realization of world peace will begin with the struggle for peace in every country.

Researchers from every field build a world that is formed from words. However, researchers must consider several questions. What are words? How are words formed? They must consider the placement of words. Where should they go? Each physical education and sports scholar communicates with the public through words. Therefore, each must take on the individual responsibility of determining what relationship these words have to the actual practice of physical education and sports. In today's world, the writing, speaking, and reading of all languages is becoming increasingly technical and/or changing for increased speed. We physical education and sports scholars must always be careful to choose words that reflect the authentic characteristics of life (which are common to all languages). Why is this so? We possess true knowledge. We do not wish to deal with fabrication. The words in the language of each country point to the actions of each country's human existence. In every country, the thing that points to the actual living, moving, acting humans in the country is language. Therefore, these words themselves (even though expressions may differ among countries) are living things. To the physical education and sports scholars of the world, I would like to stress the danger that arises when one takes words lightly. These words will become dead words, and such research will become a fabrication.

In universities today, doctorate degrees that certify authority are awarded in all academic fields. In the future, however, we will go on to award doctorate degrees in our field, namely physical education and sports studies, which will carry similar authority. Meanwhile, we must make distinctions in the types of doctorate degrees. There will be three types of doctorate degrees. The first is the doctorate degree that reflects individual characteristics. In this case, the university will decide on the number of degrees it will award, and these degrees will be awarded on the basis of a thesis presentation at a meeting of professors. This doctorate degree will be in no way based on how the research is responsible to society or the nation. It will be simply an evaluation of the individual's ability. Thus, this type of doctorate degree will be given without creating any value for society or for the nation. The second type will be the national doctorate degree. This type of degree does not exist in any field today, yet the nature of this degree would contribute to development and peace of individual countries. In fact, people with this type of doctorate should be called "living national treasures." In the future, our physical education and sports studies doctorate will be this type of degree. We cannot recognize degrees awarded by universities because these are individualistic degrees. The physical education and sports studies doctorate degree will be given for research that has national importance. The third and final type of degree will be the world doctorate. This kind of doctorate will be awarded for research that contributes to world peace and the development of humanity. The Nobel Prize given in Sweden is an example of this type. This type of degree will be the most respected doctorate, and it will mark a leader of humanity. In the future, we will award this type of physical education and sports studies doctorate degree. Therefore, there will be two types of physical education and sports studies doctorate degrees: the national doctorate degree and the world doctorate degree. These will be awarded based on a thorough review by national and world physical education and sports academies to outstanding physical education and sports scholars. When the physical education and sports studies doctorate degree is awarded, the national flag should be hoisted and the national anthem should be played as part of the ceremony (as is the case in the practice of sports). Thus, the physical education and sports studies doctorate degree will not simply be exclusive to universities, but will have an open quality.

I would like to form an organization to award the physical education and sports studies doctorate degree impartially to physical education and sports scholars who contribute to peace. Thus, the requirements for this award will be related to whether or not, through research in any of the fields within physical education and sports studies, the scholar contributes to national and world peace.

Today, it seems that physical education and sports scholars have forgotten the vitally important word "peace." These people will never amount to true physical education and sports scholars. Furthermore, the chaotic research that results from individualistic motivation can never lead to true peace. Such things are on the same level as the world of animals, in which wildness comes from individualistic desires. In the practice of sports, there are rules to insure peace. Likewise, there are rules of peace for physical education and sports research in every country in the world. Without these, we could not form a true physical education and sports psychology, a true physical education and sports physiology, a true physical education and sports sociology, a true physical education and sports philosophy, a true physical education and sports history, etc., in each country. All would become barren, fictitious academic fields. We would like to promote the establishment of physical education and sports studies as a true scholarly pursuit. We would like this to be an academic field that is recognized around the world and is important to the nation, to the world, to the IOC (International Olympic Committee) and to each country's national organizations.

From here, I will go on to develop the "Theory of Physical Education and Sports Studies for the Achievement of Peace" and the partial theories within it. Once this theory is complete, I would like to work to start a peace movement, and to build physical education and sports academies in every country and one central World Physical Education and Sports Academy. Thus, physical education and sports studies will be an academic field that, in every country and in the world, is a study of peace. Research will be conducted with a valid reason, and it will be independent from other academic areas. It is this kind of physical education and sports studies that will leave its mark in human history. I believe that we can expect the importance and necessity of physical education and sports studies to be understood by the education ministries of every country in the world, by the IOC, by other sports organizations, and by scholars in other fields. "Human progress and harmony"–these words are relevant for all of human eternity. In the future, the world's physical education and sports scholars must strive to make them a reality.

We would like to find the true elite of the world's physical education and, sports scholars who contribute to national and world peace. In the future, we will award the Physical Education and Sports Doctorate Degree (world doctorate) at the World Physical Education and Sports Academy once every four years (in the same manner as is practiced in Olympic competition). The award will be competitive and based on a thorough review, and it will take place before a large audience. Those who are awarded the degree will become the leaders of the world's physical education and sports scholars and the leaders for peace. With the birth of the world doctorate degree in physical education and sports studies, we will be able to fulfill our one true desire–the realization of world peace. We will choose these world doctors from America, Canada, France, West Germany, Italy, Japan, Sweden, Denmark, China, the Soviet Union, and from all countries alike based on valid evaluation standards. I will not stop hoping and praying for the day when this is realized.

Notes on the Human

The following relates to the concept of the word "human" and the character of the word "human," which appears in this thesis.

Biologically speaking, the human is part of the classification group called mammals. It is completely separate from all other living things, such as animals, plants, birds, insects, fish and seaweeds. If one compares the human to other living things, the form of the body and the ability to use things such as fire and language are distinctions it possesses. In America there is American English, in China, Chinese, in the Soviet Union, Russian, in Japan, Japanese, in France, French, in England, English, etc. In the languages of every country in the world, there exist unique kinds of words created by the people in each country. When these various kinds of words (or languages) are used, they become living entities. Of course, there are many expressions found around the world that relate to the expression of the word "human." At the same time, the languages of every country are proof of the existence of the living human, and they are vital elements to the human in every country.

The human has formed a society in which the humans are divided on the Earth into nationalities. These nations form all the countries of the world. In this thesis, I use the word "human." I intend it to be a word that refers directly to the entirety of the humans on the Earth in every country in the world–all humans living now. These humans are divided also by sex, age, race, regional differences, occupation, etc. However, at the same time, this word is a word that can unify all of these dividing differences. Therefore, the word "human" is a word that acts dynamically, coming and going between the two extremes of the philosophical, abstract dimension and the scientific, realistic dimension. It refers to the naked human that exists in reality and does not include things such as glasses, underwear, coats, socks, shoes, etc. Similarly, natural materials needed for human life, such as air and water, are not included in the word "human."

Of course, there is also the word "person," which refers to the individual human. This word refers to each individual, and does not, therefore, refer to the entirety of humans on the earth.

I have used the word "human," based on perceptive intuition, as a method to grasp the entirety of the human living in every country in the world in reality. Therefore, I never intend to use the word "human" in this thesis in a meaningless, careless way.

Part I

Theory of International Ball Game Studies for the Achievement of Peace

1

A Word from the Author

The term *ball human* is a symbolic term that works toward the achievement of national peace and world peace. We, the world's physical education and sports scholars, must treat this word as dearly as our own lives. This is because without the existence of the ball human, none of the language concerning the ball game and research concerning the ball game could be formed. The existence builds and determines it all. The term *ball human* is the universal language of the world's physical education and sports scholars. It is a specialized term–even a holy term.

I present this paper for the benefit of all the physical education and sports scholars of each of the world's nations alike.

2

Establishing the Hypothesis for Creating Ball Game Studies

The following are the fundamental motives for attempting to create the Theory of International Physical Education and Sports Studies for the Achievement of Peace:

1. Why, in the scholastic physical education programs of the education ministries of each country in the world, are teachers using all types of ball games as the educational resource to lead students?

2. Why are all types of ball games being brought together and performed at the Olympics founded by Baron Pierre de Coubertin of France?

3. Why are the physical education and sports researchers of each country in the world conducting research concerning all types of ball games?

4. Why are physical education teachers and physical education and sports researchers of every country in the world conducting classes in every school concerning the theory of all types of ball games?

5. Why should research concerning ball games be considered physical education studies or sports studies research?

6. Why is research concerning ball games worthy of a physical education and sports studies doctorate degree?

Presently, there exists no theory from the world's physical education and sports studies research that can answer these fundamental problems of ball game research. I have been speculating about such a fundamental theory and principles of physical education and sports studies research, and I believe that this is a very important problem for which a solution must be found. Therefore, I have undertaken this task. By pointedly asking myself these questions and trying to answer them, and from the reality and dialogue of ball games, I have endeavored to construct this theory. These problems, which are the motives for the research and contemplation I have undertaken, are vitally important and are the fundamental driving force behind the research and contemplation.

Here, in order to ask myself and answer the question "What are all types of ball games?" and, more generally, "What is a ball game?", I have formed the following hypothesis. Specifically, when a human does a ball game, *the human does not become a human–the human becomes a ball human.*[*] This new term (which will become a specialized term used among physical education and sports scholars) has been created in order to convert terms such as ball game and terms included in it (soccer, rugby, tennis, baseball, basketball, etc.) into moving, living words. Also, the world's physical education teachers take their responsibilities from the social reality of ball games being taught by sports leaders to sports students and followers.

Also in this document, I have used the word *movement human*. When we perceive the phenomenon of the ball game, we see people moving. In order to express the existence of the moving human being (apart from the technique one may have in one's arms and legs) in one noun phrase, we say *movement human*. This term refers to the entire existence of the human (individual) and some other (another person or something else) dynamically working together in both a passive and active relationship.

The term *ball human* is used to collectively represent all of the various types of ball humans, such as the soccer ball human, rugby ball human, water polo human, basketball human, golf ball human, volleyball human, baseball human, etc. Each of these terms refers directly to the existence of the working relationship between a human and a ball in each type of ball game. It is this relationship, too, which gives life to and maintains the socially significant term *ball game*.

---

[*] As a reason for the formation of the hypothesis, I believe that to do a ball game is to do a ball game, and to do a ball game is *not* no doing a ball game. *To do is to become.*

Next, I would like to explain in detail to what it is exactly that the term *ball human* refers.

The object to which the words *ball human* refer is the entirety of the working relationship between a movement ball and a movement human in the phenomenon of the ball game or in the phenomenon in which a ball is dealt with. In the world of the ball game, the movement human and the movement ball together make up the ball human. In this situation, the movement human is a *movement human* related to a movement ball and the movement ball is a ball human related to a movement human. Therefore, the two share a common point which connects them together. Specifically, this common point is the existential form in which the ball human works together in mutual independence and in certain aspects moves in a uniform motion. However, if we look objectively, we can divide the ball human into a ball human as a ball movement and a ball human as a movement human.

Therefore, in presenting the theory, in order to refer directly to both the ball human as a movement human and the ball human as a ball movement sides, we will use the term *ball human* for simplification. Only when we wish to make an explicit distinction between the two sides we use the expression "ball human as a movement human and ball human as a ball movement." Therefore, the expression, *ball human* refers to both the ball movement and the movement human sides of the ball game.

There were many reasons for the creation of the special term *ball human*, but the most important of these is the need to distinguish the general human existence from the existence experienced in the special world in which ball games are dealt with in physical education and sports studies, and to make this special independence clear. In addition, it serves to help construct theories (ball game studies) to explain the unique practice of ball games.

The next matter with which we must concern ourselves is the development of all types of ball game phenomena and phenomena that involve treatment of a ball in every country in the world. Specifically, in what form does this living phenomenon appear to our eyes? In other words, which actions in the living phenomenon of the ball game are essential and which are nonessential? Understanding this diction and

6

synthesis will lead to a clear insight into this living phenomenon.

In order to answer these questions, I will examine the living phenomenon of the ball game itself, relying on intuitive analysis and the integrated judgment method. As was stated in the hypothesis, the essence of the existence of the living phenomenon of the ball game and the phenomena in which a ball is dealt with, and the non-essence of that existence (auxiliary actions to the existential essence), are manifested in the various aspects of the ball human, such as the track and field human, the swimming human, the dance human, the skating human, etc. (*See* Figure 1.) These are, in other words, all the essential structural elements that form the living phenomenon of the ball game. I will deal in more detail in the future with the track and field human in terms of track and field studies, the dance human in terms of dance studies, the martial arts human in terms of martial arts studies, the swimming human in terms of swimming studies, etc., but for now I leave only this simplified explanation.

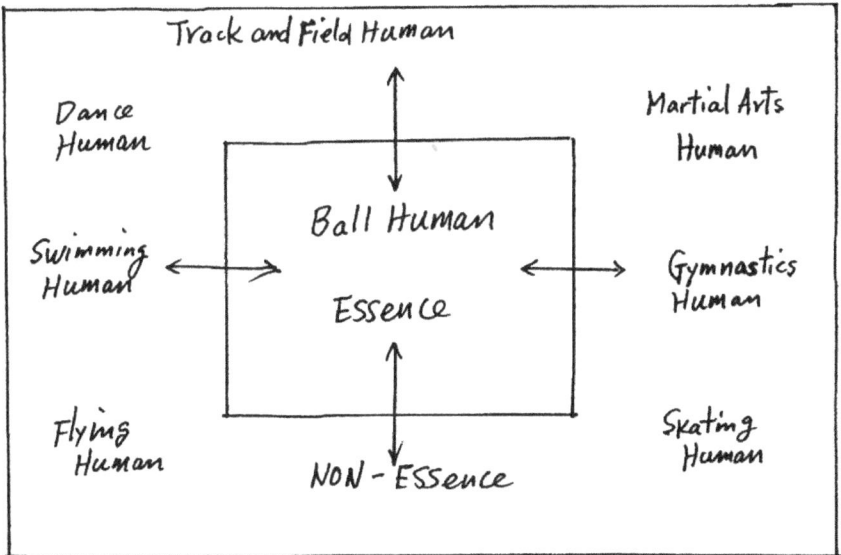

Figure 1. Formation Elements of the Living Phenomenon of the Ball Game

If we analyze the primary factors that form the movement relying on our perceptions of the ball game phenomenon and then integrate these back together, we can come to understand the movement. For example, if we look at the action of the ball human, we see that it acts on the ground, water, equipment, an image, etc., to form the living phenomenon of the ball game. In the instant the ball human acts in relation to the ground, he/she begins to exist as a track and field human. The instant the ball human acts in relation to another person, he begins to exist as a martial arts human. Furthermore, the instant the ball human acts toward a model image, he begins to exist as a dance human. These are the auxiliary actions in the living phenomenon of the ball game that create motion, and that act indirectly on the movement of the ball human.

In order to determine if Figure 1 is true or false, let us try to return to the living phenomenon (fact) of each type of ball game. For instance, to explain the living phenomenon of the water polo game using this graph, we can say that the actions of the water polo human in the water polo game appear as the existential essence. At the same time, however, the phenomenon appears as a composition of transient aspects of the non-essential, such as the swimming human, the martial arts human, the dance human, the track and field human, etc. More specifically, the phenomenon of the water polo human is most importantly the actions of the water polo ball and the actions of the human. However, this water polo human is also in dynamic contact with the water, a property of the swimming human. The living phenomenon of the water polo game also involves the actions of the relationships between the water polo human and the floor of the pool (surface), the water polo human and images, and between the water polo human (self) and water polo human (other). The determining factors in this explanation are based on perceptive insight and the variations in the flow of the water polo game, but, above all, it is determined by the actions of the water polo human–the movement of the water polo ball and the movement human.

Therefore, it is possible to say that all of the living phenomena of the various types of ball games and games that deal with balls can be found in every country in the world formed from a mixture of the characteristics of the living phenomena of the ball human, the track and field human, the swimming human, the dance human, the skating human, the martial arts human, etc. Most important, all are formed from the existential essence of the ball human, namely the living actions of the ball human that determine the process and results of the ball game. As evidence for this, the points scored in a game, which depend upon the actions of the ball human in the ball game, provide dynamic variation to the aspects of the phenomenon and the result of the game is determined by them. In addition, the many words related to the actions of the ball human also provide support.

I would like to put this idea (that the phenomenon of the ball game is the mutual actions of the ball and the human, namely the ball human) in the form of a hypothesis. However, in order to do this I must provide some clear evidence that is able to confirm that this is the existential essence in the phenomenon of the ball game. This would be the factual grounds for the formation of these words. In order to speak scientifically about the phenomenon of the ball game and phenomena in which a ball is dealt with, we must make this existential essence that will be the object of the analysis very clear. In other words, it is necessary to confirm whether or not the term *ball human* is a term that possesses realistic qualities in the phenomenon of the ball game.

Thus, I began to think that I could incorporate this method into an ontology of the ball human. In other words, using the term *ball human*, I will explain in detail the reality of the ball game. Thus, should it be possible to prove this hypothesis, the term ball human would be the existential essence in the phenomenon of the ball game and it would become specialized terminology whose use would be required any time ball game research is being conducted. Further- more, we would begin down the road toward the construction of a theory of ball game studies dealing with the entirety of practice. It would be possible to advance the theory by means of a teleology and a methodology, and finally, to form Ball Game Theory (World United and Different). A distinction would be made between the aspects of ball game studies that affect the daily lives of average humans and special areas of ball game studies. When names are given to these boundaries, ball games studies will be formed.

I have ascertained that the existence of the ball human can be grasped as three aspects, and in this way I hope to make this existence clear. Specifically, these are the social existence of the ball human, the educational existence of the ball human, and the movement-cultural existence of the ball human. These all point to the fact that, in every country in the world, the ball human exists in many ways and forms a special world. I will begin my undertaking from my understanding of the existence of this ball human–the ball human that exists in every country in the world.

3

The Movement-Cultural Ontology
of the Ball Human

Movement-culture becomes ingrained in the ball human, and the ball human exists possessing movement-cultural aspects. This comes from a connotative structure and a denotative structure. Together they maintain independent functions while living and existing as a whole.

THE CONNOTATIVE STRUCTURE

The ball human as a movement human is organically composed with a head, torso, hands, and feet. Internally, he is composed of muscles, bones, organs, a brain, etc. that all rely on blood for their actions. However, the ball human as a ball movement is actually made of many materials, such as a certain amount of air, and various other objects, all of which will be acted upon by the human being's life energy. These are based on factors of nature, which include gravity, temperature, climate, sunshine, etc., and artificial factors, which include gymnasiums, ground, lighting, etc., and they act on individual or group behavior and skill. However, these factors act together with factors dependent on the ball human as a movement human himself, such as perception, thought, emotion, etc. Therefore, the ball human as a movement human exists as a complex synthesis of the various factors that make up each human.

As individual actions, the two sides (the ball human as a movement human and the ball human as a ball movement) approach each other, come into contact, and separate from one another. These actions consist of various types, such as receiving, throwing, grasping, kicking, batting, running, walking, jumping, sliding, pushing, hitting, holding, etc.

As group actions, the two sides (the ball human as a movement human and the ball human as a ball movement) approach each other, come into contact, and separate from one another. These group actions consist of various types, such as yelling, using signals, watching, etc.

The actions of individual and group technical skills are based on the actions of the eyes, ears, tongue, skin, etc. of the ball human as a movement human and the actions of bones, bowels, and organs such as the heart, lungs, etc. Also included are the actions of the cerebrum, the midbrain, and the cerebellum, i.e., external senses such as sight, hearing, taste, touch and smell, and internal perceptions from the organs, bones, muscles, brain, etc. Finally, the actions of thought, emotion, etc. also contribute. In other words, while the "sensation/ thought/emotion" system's parts have independent functions, they are organically and dynamically related and participate in the skilled actions of the ball human as a movement human. In making value judgments about skilled actions, such as good/bad, achieved/not achieved, the ball human as a movement human relies greatly on the actions of this "sensation/thought/emotion" system. For example, decisions and conflicts such as "my head hurts/keep playing hard," "tired/time to quit," "the ball has come/go for a shot," "the ball has come/go for a catch," "I see a friend/try my best," "my Achilles tendon hurts/try even harder," etc., point to the dynamic actions of "sensation/thought/emotion," "sensation/emotion," "sensation/ thought," "thought/sensation," "emotion/sensation," "emotion/thought/ sensation," and so on.

THE DENOTATIVE STRUCTURE

The ball human as a movement human exists in various movement-cultural aspects. If we were to classify these movement-cultural aspects, we could classify them into the following four types.

The first type includes ball games in which the ball separates from the human, such as bowling, golf, gateball, etc.

The second type includes ball games in which the action of the human and the ball are mutually disjunctive and conjunctive, such as table tennis, tennis, etc.

While types one and two both deal with individualistic movement-cultural properties, both types three and four deal with movement-

12

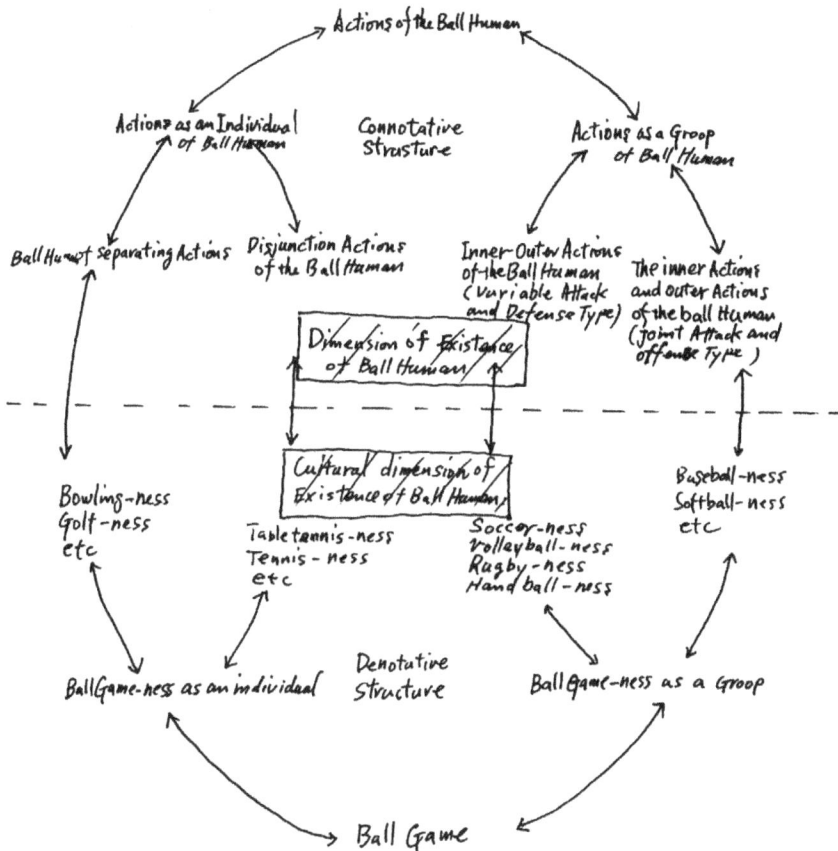

Figure 2. The Movement-cultural Existence of the Ball Human

cultural properties that are group-oriented.

The third type includes ball games in which whether or not one of the ball humans as a movement human in the group is handling the ball determines whether the group is on offense or defense. Ball games such as volleyball, soccer, handball, rugby, and basketball fall into this category.

The fourth type includes ball games in which whether or not one of the ball humans as a movement human in the group is handling the ball has no relation to whether the group is on offense or defense. This category includes baseball, softball, cricket, etc.

In this manner, we can classify the movement-cultural existence of every ball game phenomenon depending on the type and substance of the actions of the ball human in it. (See Figure 2.) However, every type of ball human as a movement human exists with its own original aspects as well. The soccer ball human has aspects of which the rugby ball human has not, and the tennis ball human exists with aspects that the table tennis ball human has not. Therefore, each ball human exists with different movement-cultural aspects and presents unique qualities.

GOLF-NESS (GOLF BALL HUMAN)

The ball human as a movement human exists in the mode of golf. For example, the ball human comes in direct and indirect contact with the golf ball, the rules of golf, golf equipment, golf terminology, golf facilities, golf clothes, golf shoes; etc., and as a golf ball human as a movement human, forms the unique world of golf,

BOWLING-NESS (BOWLING BALL HUMAN)

The ball human as a movement human exists in the mode of bowling. For example, he comes in direct and indirect contact with the bowling ball, the rules of bowling, bowling equipment, bowling terminology, bowling facilities, bowling clothes, etc., and as a bowling ball human as a movement human, forms the unique world of bowling.

TENNIS-NESS (TENNIS BALL HUMAN)

The ball human as a movement human exists in the mode of tennis. For example, he comes in direct and indirect contact with the tennis ball, the rules of tennis, tennis equipment, tennis terminology, tennis facilities, tennis clothes, etc., and as a tennis ball human as a movement human, forms the unique world of tennis.

TABLE TENNIS-NESS (TABLE TENNIS HUMAN)

The ball human as a movement human exists in the mode of table tennis. For example, he comes in direct and indirect contact with the ping-pong ball, the rules of table tennis, table tennis equipment, table tennis terminology, table tennis facilities, table tennis clothes, etc., and as a table tennis ball human as a movement human, forms the unique world of table tennis.

SOCCER-NESS (SOCCER BALL HUMAN)

The ball human as a movement human exists in the mode of soccer. For example, he comes in direct and indirect contact with the soccer ball, the rules of soccer, soccer equipment, soccer terminology, soccer facilities, soccer clothes, etc., and as a soccer ball human as a movement human, forms the unique world of soccer.

HANDBALL-NESS (HANDBALL HUMAN)

The ball human as a movement human exists in the mode of handball. For example, he comes in direct and indirect contact with the handball, the rules of handball, handball equipment, handball terminology, handball facilities, handball clothes, etc., and as a handball human as a movement human, forms the unique world of handball.

BASKETBALL-NESS (BASKETBALL HUMAN)

The ball human as a movement human exists in the mode of

basketball. For example, he comes in direct and indirect contact with the basketball, the rules of basketball, basketball equipment, basketball terminology, basketball facilities, basketball clothes, etc., and as a basketball human as a movement human, forms the unique world of basketball.

VOLLEYBALL-NESS (VOLLEYBALL HUMAN)

The ball human as a movement human exists in the mode of volleyball. For example, he comes in direct and indirect contact with the volleyball, the rules of volleyball, volleyball equipment, volleyball terminology, volleyball facilities, volleyball clothes, etc., and as a volleyball human as a movement human, forms the unique world of volleyball.

RUGBY-NESS (RUGBY BALL HUMAN)

The ball human as a movement human exists in the mode of rugby. For example, he comes in direct and indirect contact with I the rugby ball, the rules of rugby, rugby equipment, rugby terminology, rugby facilities, rugby clothes, etc., and as a rugby ball human as a movement human, forms the unique world of rugby.

WATER POLO-NESS (WATER POLO HUMAN)

The ball human as a movement human exists in the mode of water polo. For example, he comes in direct and indirect contact with the rules of water polo, water polo equipment, water polo terminology, water polo facilities, water polo clothes, etc., and as a water polo human as a movement human, forms the unique world of water polo.

HOCKEY-NESS (HOCKEY HUMAN)

The ball human as a movement human exists in the mode of hockey. For example, he comes in direct and indirect contact with the hockey puck (ball), the rules of hockey, hockey equipment, hockey terminology, hockey facilities, hockey clothes, etc., and as a hockey human as a movement human, forms the unique world of hockey.

BASEBALL-NESS (BASEBALL HUMAN)

The ball human as a movement human exists in the mode of baseball. For example, he comes in direct and indirect contact with the baseball, the rules of baseball, baseball equipment, baseball terminology, baseball facilities, baseball clothes, etc., and as a baseball human as a movement human, forms the unique world of baseball.

SOFTBALL-NESS (SOFTBALL HUMAN)

The ball human as a movement human exists in the mode of softball. For example, he comes in direct and indirect contact with the softball, the rules of softball, softball equipment, softball terminology, softball facilities, softball clothes, etc., and as a softball human as a movement human, forms the unique world of softball.

In addition, as recently developed movement-culture, there are several games which have been introduced, such as portball, gateball, etc., each with its own unique movement-cultural world. In this way, the ball human as a movement human exists in all the various movement-cultural aspects in every country in the world. In America as Americans, in the Soviet Union as Soviets, and in Japan as Japanese, the ball human exists in these various movement-cultural aspects. Furthermore, it can be assumed that in the future the number of movement-cultural aspects of the ball human as a movement human will increase further, and new names for these may certainly be introduced as well.

4

The Educational Ontology of the
Ball Human

In the special society of physical education in every country in the world, the ball human as a movement human exists possessing a "physical education human" side. Every type of ball game is evaluated educationally. Certainly, opinions are formed about whether a ball game builds strength, develops character, fosters mental growth, fosters creativity, etc. The educational existence of the ball human as a movement human comes from a connotative structure and a denotative structure. Each works based on an independent structure, and as a whole they educationally exist.

THE CONNOTATIVE STRUCTURE

In order to make clear the actions of the ball human, we will analyze them and use integrated judgment, by both looking from the actions of the ball human toward the living energy and from the living energy toward the actions of the ball human. In this manner, we can fully grasp the entire substance of the actions of the ball human. We have some factors that are expressed, such as physical condition, body strength, flexibility, etc., while in contrast, some factors are expressive, such as the mind, soul, character, personality, condition of character, morale, flexibility, etc. These factors work in a living, separate manner, and the actions of the ball human are the integration of all of these living elements. By using these words to inquire about the nature of the actions of the ball human, we can elucidate the concept of the ball human. Therefore, these words refer to the various partial factors that make up the ball human, and they are living words. The source of these words is based upon the supply and demand of living energy produced by the unification (digestion, oxidation) that takes place inside the individual of the mutually conflicting elements

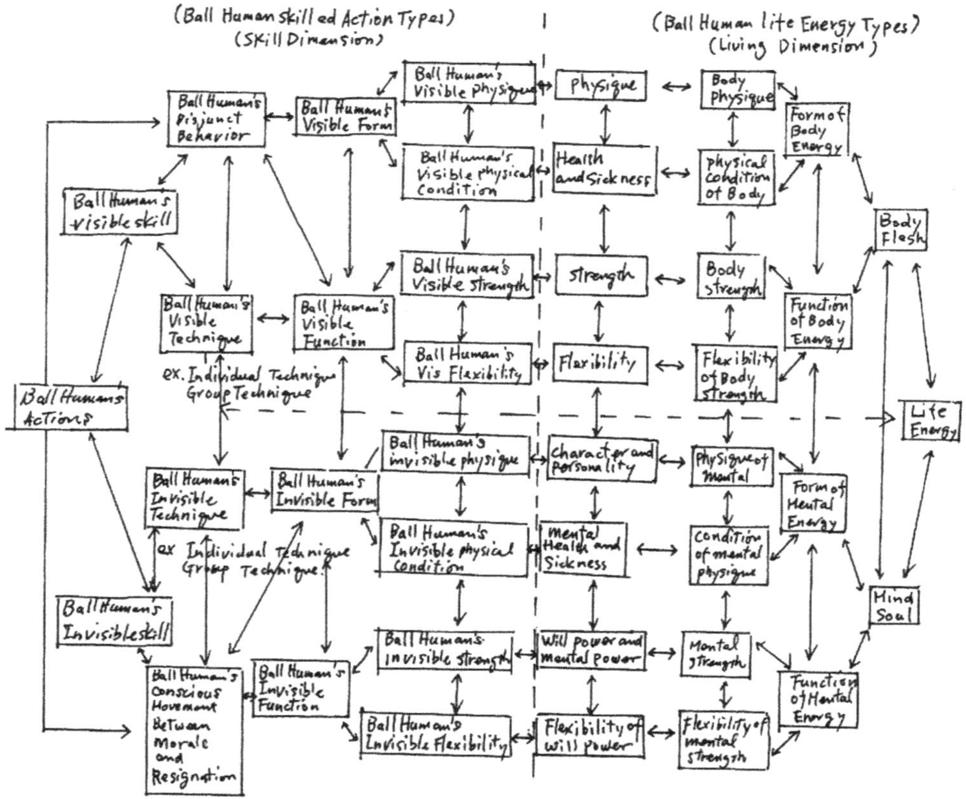

Figure 3. Action Types of the Ball Human

19

of air, food, and the existence of the ball human. In other words, the source is the transformation of the various elements, such as body, body strength, flexibility, physique, physical condition, mind, soul, morale, flexibility, personality, condition of character, etc., into a living entity. Therefore, the words body, body strength, flexibility, physique, physical condition, mind, soul, morale, flexibility, personality, and condition of character are all living words, and are words that have come to refer to reality.

On the other hand, we have said that the action of the ball human is formed from a synthesis of the various types of actions of the ball human expressed as mind, body, soul, physique, physical condition, body strength, flexibility, personality, condition of character, morale and flexibility, yet it should be noted that in our analysis of the actions of the ball human we said that there is both a ball movement and a movement human side to the ball human, with mutually different objects. Since this is the case, it may not be appropriate to use the same type of language to explain both. However, based on the common point of view that both share as the ball human, we will use the same language to explain them.

The analysis and synthesis of these two sides, the ball human as a movement human and the ball human as a ball movement, are described by Figure 3 and Figure 4.

Also making up the actions of the ball human are skilled actions, which express technique. However, if we analyze these skilled actions, we can see that they are made up of actions of the conduct of the ball human and the substance of the kind of technique being expressed. In other words, the actions of the conduct of the ball human, together with the substance of the technique, make up the reality of the skilled actions of the ball human and exist united in reality. These exist in a relationship that is mutually life giving and enlivened, creating the phenomenon of the skilled existence of the ball human.

Figure 4. The Types and Content of the Actions of the *Ball Human*

I.   The visible physique of the ball human
   • Ball's size, weight, material, color, shape, etc.

- Human's body weight, height, arm extension, height when sitting, etc.
II. The condition of the visible physique of the ball human
   - Quality of firmness of the ball, amount of air, bounce, etc.
   - Condition of the human body, qulaity of organs
III. The visible physical strength of the ball human
   - Endurability and speed ability of the ball–time strength
   - Endurability and speed ability of the ball–space strength
   - Endurability and speed ability of the human–time strength
   - Endurability and speed ability of the human–space strength
IV. The visible flexibility of the ball human
   - The effective physical ability and flexibility of the ball in response to the game
   - The effective physical ability and flexibility of the human in response to the game
V. The effective physical ability and flexibility of the human in response to the game

----

VI. The invisible physique of the ball human
   - Introversion and extroversion of the ball
   - Introversion and extroversion of the human
VII. The condition of the invisible physique of the *ball human*
   - Quality of the character of the ball
   - Quality of the character of the human
VIII. The invisible physical strength of the ball human
   - Endurability and speedability of the moreale of the ball–time strength
   - Endurability and speedability of the moreale of the ball–space strength
   - Endurability and speedability of the moreale of the human–time strength
   - Endurability and speedability of the moreale of the human–space strength

IX. The invisible flexibility of the ball human
  • The flexibility of the morale of the ball
  • The flexibility of the morale of the human

THE DENOTATIVE STRUCTURE

In regard to the denotative structure of the educational existence of the ball human, I have attempted some analytical speculation that will explain it as shown in Figure 5.

Figure 5. The Educational Existence of the Ball Human

	First Analysis	Second Analysis
subjective/objective, objective/subjective dynamic fact	Entire expression of ball human (social standpoint)	Sociality (objective) Discovery-ness (subjective)
Educational phenomenon of the ball human	Partial expression of ball human (Individual standpoint)	Cooperativeness (objective) Creativity (subjective)

SOCIALITY

The ball human functions in the special society of the ball game. However, in order to create this special society, it must work by accepting and approving all of the factors. Specifically, the ball human as a movement human that takes on the special social role of "player" acts both socially and morally. The ball human as a movement human acts in participation with the humans that take on the social roles of judges, teachers, leaders, etc., and even with things that are set up for the purpose of becoming a ball human as a movement human, such as unique facilities, equipment, rules, etc. In this manner, the phenomenon of the ball game is when, as the ball human as a movement human is enlarged from some person to something and from something to some person, it acts both socially and morally. However, while the sociality of the ball human as a movement human provides the nature of a special sociality, in order that ball games occur in general society, it exists in the twofold relationship with general society and the special society of the ball game.

DISCOVERY-NESS

The ball human as a movement human acts creatively. At the same time, the ball human as a ball movement also acts creatively. In the actions of the ball human, there are situations in which new technical content or form, of which no similar example existed in the past, are added. These new techniques are conceptualized and given special names. This itself points to the discovery-ness of the ball human. For example, names such as *cut-in play, time-difference offense, screen play, three-two defense,* etc., point to the discovery-ness of the ball human. Also, in the beginning of the nineteenth century, we can see a boy in physical education history named William Webb Ellis who was in a rugby school in England. According to him, the conduct of acting as a football human suddenly brought about the birth of the rugby ball human. In this way, there are situations in which a new ball human is given existence and movement-cultural history is formed. The discovery-ness of the ball human consists of both the creative and historical expansion aspects of these actions.

COOPERATIVENESS

In the phenomenon of the ball game and the phenomena in which a ball is dealt with, there are many cases in which the ball human acts in a group. In these cases, cooperative intentions are demanded of the ball human. This cooperativeness depends on the mutual relationship between acting ball humans that have taken on the social role of the "player," and therefore this is a social action. In the cooperativeness of the ball human, there is cooperativeness from a unified standpoint, and cooperativeness from a different standpoint. For example, the general factors of the school associated with the individual ball human, the region, age, sex, etc. may be identical or different. Also, the various factors of the special standpoint of the ball game such as skill level of the ball human the "player" role, companions, etc. may be identical or different.

In this way, the actions of the cooperativeness of the ball human exist as the nature of the identities and differences of general things and the identities and differences of the special things limited only to the ball game. So if we try to limit it to only the cooperativeness in the special society of the ball game, the cooperativeness of identity recognition of the ball human is based on the recognition of technical standpoint, and the cooperativeness of difference recognition is based on the recognition of existential standpoint.

CREATIVITY

The ball human, in the living, always-changing space of the ball game, acts while at every moment being faced with the problem, "In what way should I best handle the ball?" The ball human as a ball movement, which has been acted on by the ball human as a movement human, is a concrete expression of the skill of the ball human as a movement human itself. It is something that indicates the level of skill. Therefore, the ball human as a ball movement demands skill from the ball human as a movement human, and conversely, the ball human as a movement human exists while demanding skill from the ball human as a ball movement. Through the skill demands of these two sides, the ball human creates. For example, the ball human as a ball movement that is thrown by the ball human as a movement human, which has taken the social role of "pitcher," approaches the ball human as a movement human, which has taken the social role of "hitter," as skill. Then, the *ball human* as a movement human tries to face this ball movement, and through the bat as an extension of the individual's body, tries to respond to the skilled action of the ball movement. As a result, the action of a strikeout, a home run, a foul, a tip, or a hit will be created.

The creativity of the ball human can be seen in the creativity of the partial cause/effect action of kicking and the action of going inside, and the action of hitting and the action of fouling. Through this partial cause/effect process, the action of winning, the action of losing, and the action of a draw are created. Creativity can be seen in the partial cause/effect actions in the entire process of the ball game, from start to finish. Furthermore, the creativity generates the subjective emotions of happiness, vexation, anger, and sorrow at every instant in the ball human as a movement human. In this manner, the ball human as a movement human and the ball human as a ball movement, in the special living space of the ball game, the unknown space of the ball game, and the regulated space of the ball game, are acting creatively in an original way. These actions bring about a reformation of the self-consciousness of the possibilities of ability in the ball human which has taken the special social role of "player." In this special society, it gives meaning to life.

In this way, the ball human educationally exists. At the same time, it exists as the educational beings in scholastic physical education in every country in the world, and is an expression of every country in the world in its existence.

5

The Social Ontology of the Ball Human

The ball human exists within general society. There it exists while possessing an aspect of social existence in which it lives trying to plan original plans. For example, from the factual phenomenon of the ball game, all kinds of words have been derived, such as "to do sports," "to do physical education," "to do recreation," etc. On the other hand, in the social actions of the ball human, there are various kinds of social language that have been created, such as "fair," "unfair," "cooperative," etc. This can be said to be implicit proof that the ball human exists socially. Concerning the social existence of the ball human, in order to grasp its factual living state as a living state, I will divide this into a connotative structure and a denotative structure and explain each. Therefore, the social existence of the ball human is the entirety of the independent actions of connotative structure and denotative structure.

THE CONNOTATIVE STRUCTURE

Let us consider the basic aspects of the actions of the ball human. In the case of the individual, it is the actions of mutual separation/contact within the ball human. In the case of the group, it is the actions of mutual separation/contact between many ball humans. In other words, the basic principle is the entirety of the motion that occurs when the ball human as a ball movement and the ball human as a movement human mutually separate, approach, and contact.

If we apply this fact to each kind of the entire phenomenon of the ball game, it will be easily understood. This is described by Figure 6.

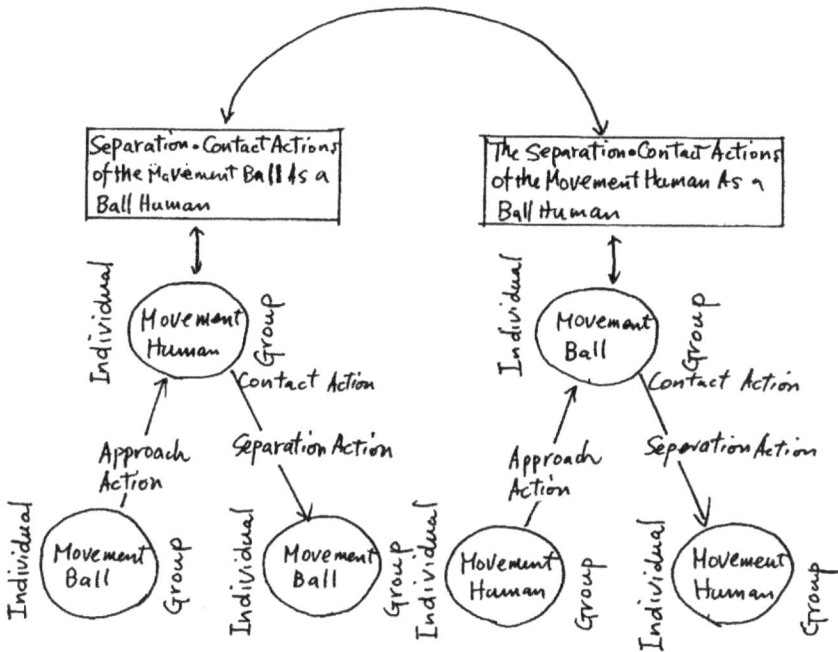

Figure 6. The Separation/Contact Actions of the Ball Human

In other words, in order to grasp this dynamic separation/contact relationship between the ball humans, one must begin by looking objectively from the actions of the body of the ball human. Meanwhile, there are also the actions of the mind of the ball human, namely the separation/contact movement of consciousness. Those actions come from the fact that when dealing with the ball, the ball human as a movement human recognizes the ball by the action of unconscious/conscious. The strength, or perhaps weakness, of the actions of the consciousness of the ball human as a movement human is located in the polarized structure of the morale and resignation of the consciousness. The strength or weakness depends throughout on the manner in which the consciousness moves between this polarization.

As the ball human as a movement human lives, breathes, and goes to the ball human as a ball movement, and as the ball human as a ball movement lives, breathes, and goes to the ball human as a movement human, the morale strengthens the consciousness. In other words, the morale strengthens the unified perception of the both sides of the ball human, the ball human as a movement human and the ball human as a ball movement, as a ball human. It also promotes the manifestation of living as a ball human. For example, in a hotly contested baseball game, the pitcher itself and each pitch that the pitcher throws come to be perceived as a unified dimension.

Because the morale is a living thing, it promotes flattering aspects, but since it is caused through the consciousness's condition of resignation, it moves to the resignation, which is a different kind of element. Primarily, the morale of the ball human is in the dimension of time, which has a passive nature and has some bad points, but in the dimension of space, it has an active nature. The morale possesses these kinds of properties.

However, the resignation of the ball human is the condition of the consciousness of the preparation steps for displaying the conscious-ness of morale. Therefore, the resignation of the ball human, in relation to the morale, is an element of denial, but on the other hand, it provides a kind of quality which serves to support morale as well. In the realm of space, the resignation of the ball human is weak and passive, but in the realm of time it is strong and active.

The connotative structure of the social existence of the ball human presents the mutual actions of separation/contact between ball humans. Objectively, the body acts by the separation/contact actions, and at the same time, subjectively, the mind acts by the separation/contact actions. Together they act as a whole. Within these actions, the changes in consciousness are acting, namely by presenting the aspects of morale and resignation.

Concerning the actions of the ball human, we use many different expressions to express them. These different expressions all rely on the aspects of the actions of the ball human. (Refer to Figure 7.)

Figure 7. Natural Expressions Related to the Actions of the Ball Human

Names of the Actions of the Ball Human Ball Movement:	Names of Actions of the Ball Human Movement Human:
going in	striking
flying	throwing
being hit	pushing
rolling	kicking
rotating	hitting
bouncing	receiving
etc.	etc.

For example, in order to make sentences for classifications within the types of ball humans, such as the actions of the soccer ball human and the baseball human, one would proceed in the following way:

The ball human as a movement human acts by kicking, the ball human as a ball movement goes into the goal. (The actions of the soccer ball human.)

The ball human as a movement human acts by striking the ball human as a ball movement goes into the grandstand. (The actions of the baseball human.)

In the above manner, the actions of the connotative structure of the ball human themselves act in an original way. At the same time, they also act with aspects of denotative structure.

THE DENOTATIVE STRUCTURE

In the following way, I have analyzed and gained insight into the denotative elements of the social existence of the ball human, and I have attempted to extract the denotative elements themselves. (See Figure 8.)

Figure 8. The Social Existence of the *ball human*

	First Analysis	Second Analysis
		Recreation-ness
		Competitiveness
	Entire expression	Sports-ess/Physical
	of the Ball Human	Education-ness
The Aspects of the		
Social Existence of		
the Ball Human		Combativeness/
		Cooperativeness
	Partial Expression	Primitiveness/
	of the Ball Human	Modernity

From the chart above, I will explain each of the social factors of the ball human listed in the second analysis.

RECREATION-NESS AND COMPETITIVENESS

First there is recreation-ness, in which the ball human amuses itself with entertaining ball games, such as when using company free time with a group of co-workers or when a family enjoys a ball game. There is also competitiveness, which includes tension of the kind of seriousness such as when competitive leagues are commissioned by the sponsorship of all kinds of competitive groups. The recreation-ness of the ball human fosters a place for the meeting of the hearts of the ball human as a movement human comrade and the ball human as a movement human and the ball human as a ball movement comrade. It is a softening aspect that pursues mutual understanding. Then there is the competitiveness, which is the aspect of the ball human where, within the rules of competition, a ball human as a movement human comrade, or perhaps a ball human as a movement human and a ball human as a ball movement comrade facing one another, act with bravery and valorous determination. The greater the scale of the competitive league, the more the spirit intensifies, and the competitiveness of the ball human appears more conspicuous. For

30

instance, this is the case in all the types of ball games in the Olympics and all types of ball games in international leagues, etc.

PHYSICAL EDUCATION-NESS–SPORTS-NESS

In the phenomenon of the ball game, based on the fundamental structure of the teacher and pupil, the educational environment and content are given in the school's gym or corresponding place. This is the physical education-ness of the ball human doing a ball game. The physical education-ness of the ball human is an educational phenomenon which depends on the sum total of the teacher and pupil. This is an aspect of the special society called *school* and an aspect of the actions of the ball human that comes from a regionally narrow scope. The student who is recognized by the school side, perhaps specially selected, from nursery school through elementary, junior high, and high school, will be acting the role of the physical education-ness of the ball human. On the other hand, the phenomenon of the ball game in general society is an expression of the sports-ness of the ball human. The sports-ness of the ball human is the aspect of the ball human in which, in the social phenomenon that relies on the sum total of leaders and followers, a wide range of many kinds of games are developed with no relevance to sex, age, or occupation. For example, when a group of mothers get together and do volleyball, there is the phenomenon of "Mama Volley." Also, there is the phenomenon of the little leagues, which are directed towards the local youth. Furthermore, there are the phenomena of professional baseball, professional soccer, etc. All of these are expressions of the sports- ness of the ball human.

COMBATIVENESS–COOPERATIVENESS

In the actions of the ball human, there are the elements of the contrasting actions of combativeness and cooperativeness. The action of a *pass* of an individual ball human as a movement human on a team of ball humans is an expression of cooperativeness. This action of the pass between companion bay humans creates a oneness of the team/individual, and builds many conscious states. It conspicuously expresses the cooperativeness of the ball human. This aspect can also

31

be seen in the phenomenon where a group does a ball game, where as actions of the ball human, the skilled actions of the ball human as an individual are sublimated to the skilled actions of the ball human as a group. Namely, when there is a lack in the skilled actions of one ball human as a movement human, it is compensated for by the skilled actions of some other ball human as a movement human as an individual. In addition, there is also the aspect in which in order for one ball human as a movement human as an individual to do skilled actions, some different ball human as a movement human as an individual tries to give assistance. In these forms, this aspect appears.

In contrast to this, there are also times when, with a stern attitude toward other ball humans, the ball human as an individual attacks the ball humans that are enemies. This is an expression of the combativeness of the ball human. It is most conspicuous in the setting of vehement competition between ball humans. Combativeness can be seen in every phenomenon of the ball game and every phenomenon in which a ball is dealt with. It is the moment when the skilled actions of the ball human as an individual are steeply opposed to the skilled actions of some other ball human as an individual and they attack each other. It also can be the moment of attack that appears between the skilled actions of ball humans of a group.

PRIMITIVENESS-MODERNITY

In the ball game or in any phenomenon in which a ball is dealt with, there is the primitiveness of the ball human, in which the ball human engages in direct body contact. In games such as volleyball, handball, soccer, rugby, basketball, tennis, table tennis, baseball, and softball, there is direct contact with the ball in the actions toward the ball human as a movement human that has taken on the role of "player," such as the situations of grasping, hitting, receiving, etc. Therefore, the primitiveness of the ball human involves giving a large, direct impact to the body of the ball human as a movement human, but the opportunities to handle the ball are relatively frequent.

On the other hand, there is an aspect of modernity of the ball human, in which in the relation between ball humans, the ball human acts by using equipment. Baseball, softball, tennis, golf, table tennis, etc. are all ball games that conspicuously express the modernity of the ball human. In the modernity of the ball human, the impact of the ball received by the body of the ball human as a movement human is small. The handling of the ball is relatively rare, and the freedom is limited.

Moreover, to say that here in the denotative structure we have come up with a comprehensive list of all of the words that refer to the social existence of the ball human would be incorrect. I have aimed only for a coordinated understanding of the social existence of the ball human, and for an understanding of it as a living existence. Furthermore, if we look at the all the various elements of the social existence of the ball human, such as the amateur-ness or professional-ness of the ball human, the fitness of the ball human, the fair play-ness of the ball human, and the playfulness of the ball human, we can see that these elements are vital elements that act to stir up the social aspects of the ball human. In this manner, in every country in the world, the ball human expresses the originality of each country and carries on a social existence. In the stream of time of past-present-future, this existence lives in the present as realistic beings, and this existence is variable and alive.

6

Generalizations from the Ontology
of the Ball Human

Up to this point, the three existences of the ball human, namely the educational, social, and movement-cultural existences, have been clearly explained. The words *ball human*, when taken as in the hypothesis, are language that refers to the existential essence of the phenomenon of the ball game and the phenomena with which a ball is dealt. In other words, we have confirmed the fact that the words *ball human* are alive and exist, forming the special expanding world of ball games and dealing with balls in every country in the world. We have also confirmed the fact that these words refer directly to a special kind of human. The ball human exists as the expression of each country in the world, in America as Americans, in the Soviet Union as Soviets, in China as Chinese, in Japan as Japanese, and in Sweden as Swedish. In the present of the ever flowing stream of past-present-future, with living and variable aspects, it exists and lives.

Now, as a result of the clear evidence of the existential essence of the ball game and the clear evidence of the existence of the ball human in the phenomenon of the ball game, the following kinds of questions can now be answered:

Question 1: What is the phenomenon of the ball game?
Answer: This is the phenomenon in which, when a human and a ball occur in the ball game, they do not become a human and a ball, but instead both sides become a ball human.

Question 2: What does it mean to do a ball game?
Answer: This is when some humans become ball humans that can be divided into, on the one hand, a movement human, and on the other hand, a ball movement.
Example:

Question #1: What is rugby?

Answer: This is when a human and a rugby ball become a rugby ball human.

Question #2: What does it mean to do rugby?

Answer: This is when the human becomes a rugby ball human that can be divided into a rugby ball movement and a movement human.

Question 3: What does it mean to do a ball game in physical education?

Answer: This is the conduct in which the human becomes a ball human as a movement human and a ball human as a ball movement, and both of these are physical education-ized and try to become physical education-ized.

Question 4: What does it mean to do a ball game in sports?

Answer: This is the conduct in which the human becomes a ball human as a movement human and a ball human as a ball movement, and both of these are sports-ized and try to become sports-ized.

Question 5: What does it mean to do a ball game in the Olympics?

Answer: This is the conduct in which the human becomes a ball human as a movement human and a ball human as a ball movement, and both of these are Olympic-ized and try to become Olympic-ized.

Question 6: What does it mean to do a ball game in recreation?

Answer: This is the conduct in which the human becomes a ball human as a movement human and a ball human as a ball movement, and both of these are recreation-ized and try to become recreation-ized.

Any other questions concerning the phenomenon of the ball game itself can be answered from the educational, social, and movement-cultural ontologies previously presented.

Furthermore, this ball human encompasses every type of ball human. Namely, it is the existence of the soccer ball human, the existence of the rugby ball human, the existence of the table tennis ball human, the existence of the tennis ball human, the existence of the handball human, the existence of the baseball human, the existence of the softball human, etc. Also, depending on the differences in sex, age, race, school, occupation, etc., the above exist as different expressions.

In the above manner, through the movement of speculation, the establishment of the ontology of the ball human, from both an abstract standpoint and a concrete standpoint, from the existence to being, and from being to existence, became possible. Here, we can generalize this system as the ontology of the ball human. Finally, while I have referred to the existence of the ball human as a special existence of the human in the ball game, I must now go on to present the existence of a purpose in the existence of the ball human. Namely, the existence of the ball human that I have presented up until now is an existence which acts in order to realize the ball human image. It is that purpose for which the existence is acting. Therefore, I must now go on to develop a presentation concerning the ball human image–the teleology of the ball human. I would like to affirm the ball human image that comes from the existence of the ball human, which exists with special aspects in the ball game.

7

The Teleology of the Ball Human

Until this point, I have contemplated the existential essence in the phenomenon of all types of ball games, namely the existence of all types of the ball human. I have clearly shown and confirmed that in every country in the world, every type of ball human exists in the world of each type of ball game. However, at the same time, this existence includes the purpose of the ball human, namely the ball human image. It is not simply the existence of the ball human, but also an existence that tries to realize the ideal image that the ball human must attain. Above all, the practice of all types of ball games that is being conducted in scholastic physical education in every country in the world is being practiced for the sake of the realization of all types of the ball human image by all types of the ball human. Also, there is the necessity for physical education and sports studies research concerning all types of ball games in every country in the world (such as physical education and sports studies philosophy, physical education and sports studies psychology, physical education and sports studies physiology, physical education and sports studies sociology, physical education and sports studies history, etc.) in order to plan the realization of the ball human image, in the practice of the ball game or practice where a ball is dealt with, in physical education.

At this point I will go on to speculate about what kind of special ideal image is meant by the purpose of the ball human, or more specifically, by the ball human image.

The ball human image is, of course, the purpose of the practice of the ball game, but it is necessary to clearly explain to what in reality it is to which this word directly refers. It refers to the ideal image in which the actions of the ball human as a movement human and the actions of the ball human as a movement human and the actions of the ball human as a ball movement in the practice of the ball game are existing together doing superior actions. The ball human image is the ideal image that is living and exists ideally from one era to the next in every country in the world. This is determined by the research of the physical education and sports theory specialists (such as physical education and sports studies philosophers, physical education and sports studies psychologists, physical education and sports studies physiologists, physical education and sports studies sociologists, physical education and sports studies historians, etc.) The words *ball human image* are referring directly to the ideal existence that adds weight, depth, size, and breadth to that acting existence.

In the nature of the substance of the ball human, there are really two different kinds of natures. Also, these two natures dynamically act together and form the firm' ball human image. The first is the part of the purpose that has a universal nature that is common, no matter what the time, no matter what the place, no matter what the country. For example, all of the superior actions of the movement human and the

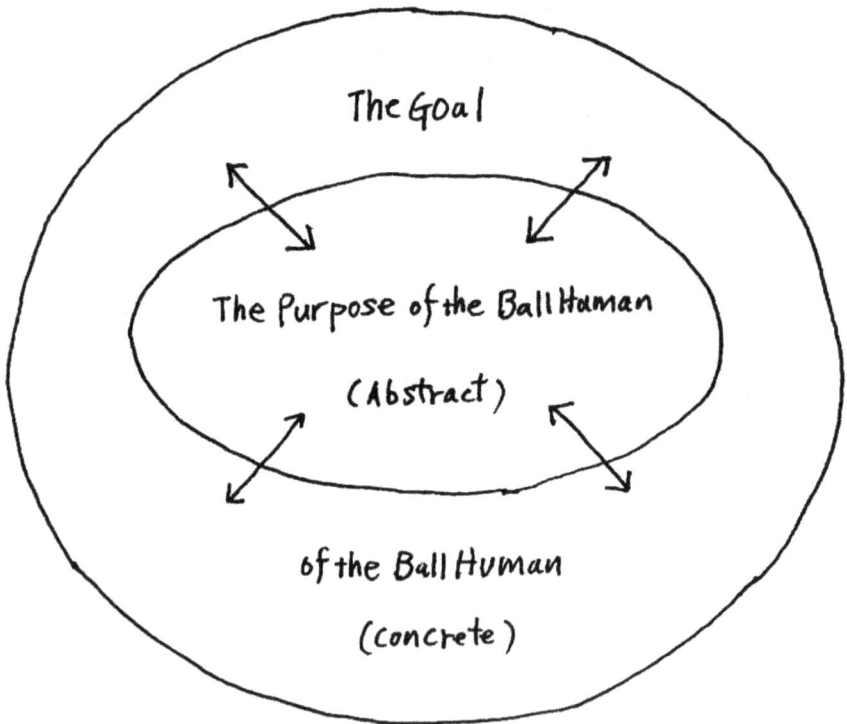

Figure 9. Constitution of the Ball Human Image

38

ball movement, in other words the attempt to realize the ball human image, even though there are differences between the histories, cultures, ideas, race, etc. of all the countries in the world, share a common universal nature.

The second is the concrete purpose of the ball human, which is variable depending on the time, the society, age, sex, and other things that are different from country to country. In every country, there is originality in history, ideas, and culture. The ball human image of a certain era in each country of the world has the aspects of that era. Furthermore, from the point of view of age, the various types of the ball human image for children are different from the various types of the ball human image for old people. From the point of view of sex, the ball human is not identical, due to the various ways of differing. Therefore, as opposed to the purpose of the universal substance of the ball human, this points to the variable, concrete purpose of the ball human. The constitution of the teleology of the ball human relies on the support/being-supported relationship between these two sides, which is a relationship that acts dynamically and mutually to support each side. The ball human image of the former is the *purpose* of the ball human, while the ball human image of the latter is the *goal* of the ball human. The difference between these words clearly points to the difference between the universal purpose and the variable purpose. Therefore, the ball human image consists of the purpose substance as its core, and that which surrounds the purpose substance is the goal substance. The dynamic relationship between them assumes the character of abstract/concrete-concrete/abstract. Because of this, the ball human image possesses unifying qualities that transcend the realities of time, nationality, age, sex, etc., but at the same time, this teleology is also one that sees those realities as realities. This can be summarized in Figure 9 (previous page).

Next, I would like to go on and explain the purpose of the ball human. Specifically, of what substance is the ball human image itself constructed? I will now explain this point.

The structure of the ball human image is made up of two types of structure: a connotative structure and a denotative structure. These form the living, unified whole. There are the actions of all of the many element images, and as a whole they act ideally. If we broadly divide these various idealistic elements, they come from the connotative structure and the denotative structure (refer to Figure 10).

THE IMAGE OF CONNOTATIVE STRUCTURE

In the actions of the ball human image, there is the image of connotative structure. This acts as the foundation of the generation of the image of denotative structure, and so this is a vitally important area. The image of connotative structure itself is formed from the various element images that become the many different ideals. It is formed from the ideal of the image of life energy that comes from physical education and sports nutrition studies and physical education and sports hygiene, the ideal of the image of the body and the image of the mind (mind-body image) that come from physical education and sports philosophy, the ideal of the image of body strength, the image of flexibility, the image of physique and the image of physical condition (the image of health) that come from physical education and sports physiology, etc. The physical education and sports studies researchers of every country in the world will go on to prove the realistic existence of the ball human. Relying on the leadership of this proof, the previous images of the connotative structure of the ball human will be concretely alive and acting ideal images. Then, in order that the physical education and sports studies researchers of every country in the world expand on the substance of the words of these various elements, and in order to promote understanding of these words as living things, the research of purpose will proceed. As a result, to the question "Why are the educational ministries of every country in the world conducting and practicing all kinds of ball games in scholastic physical education?" one will be able to provide a direct answer from the various fields of physical education and sports studies, namely physical education and sports philosophy, physical education and sports psychology, physical education and sports physiology, physical education and sports sociology, physical education and sports history, etc. For example, from physical education and sports philosophy, all types of ball games are practiced in scholastic physical education in order to realize the image of the mind and body of all types of the ball human image. The content of the image of the mind and body can be explained relying on the research of physical education and sports philosophers. Of the content of the partial element images presented here, all are ideal content that are drawn from the proof of the all of the specialist researchers in physical education and sports studies. And at the same time, in the space of the various elements in the image of connotative structure, they are things that are doing superior actions.

Also, these are the various elements that do superior actions in the image of the denotative structure as well. For example, "the image of body strength" is the superior inner actions of body strength itself, acting in superior actions in relation to the various elements, such as morale, flexibility, cooperativeness, competitiveness, physical condition, creativeness, etc.

As is shown above, the image of the connotative structure in the ball human image is the entirety of the various elements of the connotative structure that have been amassed by the physical education and sports studies researchers in every country in the world and the physical education and sports studies research of every era. However, this image of connotative structure acts not only in the image of connotative structure, but is also an image of connotative structure that works in the image of denotative structure. So, what kind of substance of ideal images make up the image of the denotative structure of the ball human? I will now go on to deal with this question.

THE IMAGE OF DENOTATIVE STRUCTURE

In the actions of the ball human image as a ball human image, there is an image of denotative structure. In the ideal image that is generated from the image of connotative structure, the origin of the formation of the image of the denotative structure is included. Inside the denotative structure itself, which acts as the denotative structure, are the actions of the various element images.

Looking from the specialized point of view of the physical education and sports sociologists and scholastic physical education, and considering the existential direction of the ball human, if an inquiry is made to determine the ideal images of that existence, then in the following way, the idealistic elements of the denotative structure become visible. The image of sports-ness, the image of physical education-ness, the image of amateur-ness, the image of professional-ness, the image of trim-ness, the image of recreation-ness, the image of teacher-ness, the image of stu- dent-ness, the image of leader-ness, the image of follower- ness, the image of manager-ness, the image of coach-ness, the image of director-ness, the image of soccer-ness, the image of tennis-ness, the image of rugby-ness, the image of water polo-ness, the image of golf-ness, the image of hand- ball-ness, the image of badminton-ness, the image of baseball-ness, the image of basketball-ness, the image of pitcher-ness, the image of keeper-ness, the image of fullback- ness, the image of server-ness, the image of right back-ness, the image of referee-ness, the image of creativeness, the image of cooperativeness, the image of competitiveness, the image of objective-ness, the image of discovery-ness, the image of subjectiveness, etc. From the above kinds of images of elements, the image of the denotative structure in the ball human image is formed. The above various images of elements are the various aspects of the ball human image, and they are things that have been culled from researchers in physical education and sports sociology and scholastic physical education. Then, the images of the various elements in the denotative structure act in a way that promotes the idealistic condition of the connotative structure, while at the same time they are the superior denotative elements that act in a way that promotes the idealistic condition of the elements in the image of the denotative structure. Therefore, each of the elements in the denotative structure themselves are elements that are superior and ad ideally.

In the above manner, the ball human image itself is the purpose of the existence of the ball human in every country in the world. Therefore, this is limited by the existence of the ball human, and in reality there is a purpose in straining to derive the ball human image from this existence. For example, in order to explain this ball human image as a ball human image in reality, we can divide the ball human image into its various types, such as the soccer ball human image, the golf ball human image, the water polo human image, the handball human image, the rugby ball human image, and so on. We can concretely express the goal of the ball human if we look, for instance, at the soccer ball human from various points of view. From the point of view of school level, there are the elementary school soccer ball human image and the high school soccer ball human image. From the point of view of sex, there are the male soccer ball human image and the female soccer ball human image. From the point of view of age, there are the ten-year-old soccer ball human image and the forty-year-old soccer ball human image. From the point of view of nationality, there are the soccer ball human image as an American, the soccer ball human image as a Japanese, the soccer ball human image as a Soviet, the soccer ball human image as a Swede, the soccer ball human image as an Australian, and so on. In other words, because the existence of all types of the ball human in every country of the world is different, the purpose of the ball human can be materialized as different goals. On the other hand, while the ball human image can make as its purpose the various unique ball human images of each country in the world, from a global, humanistic, common point of view, it can also present a purpose that is the ball human image as a world citizen. Provided that the existence of all types of the ball human practicing all kinds of ball games in all places around the world can be confirmed, this purpose can be erected as a common purpose of all types of the world citizen, or perhaps mankind, ball human image.

Above I have presented the purpose of the ball human, or more specifically, the substance of the ball human image (limited to only the important substance necessary in Ball Game theory). As a result, we have reached a point at which the following kinds of questions can be answered:

Question 1: Why are the educational ministries of every country in the world practicing all types of ball games scholastic physical education?
Answer: All types of ball games are being practiced in scholastic physical education in every country in the world in order to realize all types of the ball human image as the peoples of every country in the world.

Question 2: Why are the educational ministries of every country in the world doing classes on the theory concerning all types of ball games in scholastic education?

Answer: This is so that in the scholastic education of every country in the world, physical education teachers will show the peaceful practice of all types of ball games to the students, and so that they will explain the practice of all types of ball games to the students and the students will understand them.

Question 3: Why is the IOC doing all types of ball games in the Olympics?

Answer: The IOC is practicing all types of ball games so that, in the Olympics, all types of the ball human image will be realized. Also, this practice will translate into world peace.

Question 4: Why are the physical education and sports researchers of every country in the world conducting research in fields such as physical education and sports psychology, physical education, and sports philosophy, physical education and sports physiology, physical education and sports history, physical education and sports sociology, etc.? Furthermore, is it necessary that they do so?

Answer: This is so that in the place of the ball game in every country in the world, the ball human image of every country in the world will be realized. This research is the guarantee of the peaceful practice of ball games in every country. Also, in order to answer the question "Why must the educational ministries of every country in the world, the IOC, and sports groups be made to recognize and practice all types of ball games?" directly from theory, this is necessary and important research. Relying on the execution of this research, the practice of ball games will be guaranteed to be a peaceful practice.

Question 5: Why must a World Physical Education and Sports Academy be established?

Answer: Relying on the development of this type of re- search, the ball human image in every country in the world and the ball human image of each age of mankind will be constructed, thus developing the guarantee of peace in every country and world peace. Also, the academy will nurture physical education and sports researchers who will contribute to peace in every country and to world peace.

Question 6: Why must a Physical Education and Sports Academy be established in every country in the world?
Answer: Physical education and sports researchers from every field are necessary to construct the ball game theory in every country and to guarantee that the practice of ball games in every country in the world is a peaceful practice. They will promote research with meaning that contributes to peace in their countries. At the same time, it is also necessary to nurture national doctorates in every country, and to nurture physical education and sports researchers who will contribute to world peace through ball game studies research in every country.

In addition, any questions concerning the purpose of formation related to all types of ball games in every country in the world can be answered from the Teleology of the Ball Human. Also, through the purpose, it is necessary to go on to develop support for peace in every country and world peace.

Furthermore, from the presentations of the Ontology and Teleology of the Ball Human in every country in the world, we must now go on to develop the Methodology of the Ball Human in every country in the world by which the existence of the ball human in every country in the world realizes the ball human image of every country in the world. This will deal with the method by which the existence of the ball human in every country in the world realizes the ball human image. The Methodology will be organically connected to the Ontology and the Teleology, and will have the unique quality that it will work together with them. This kind of undertaking will work through the realization of the establishment of universal ball game theory, which unites all countries in the world and accepts differences between all countries in the world.

8

The Methodology of the Ball Human

The methodology of the Ball Human is an original theoretical area that deals with both the movement human and the ball movement sides of the phenomenon of all types of ball games. These two sides, which are referred to directly by the term "ball human," can be said to be able to, depending on how they work together to emphasize an intent on harmony, realize the ball human image. For example, if we emphasize the ball movement, only the ability required for the ball movement is required of the movement human. On the other hand, if we emphasize the movement human, only the ability required for the movement human is required of the ball movement. Therefore, achieving the required ability that is possible when both sides accept each other's demands is imperative. This type of method is the only advanced method by which the ball human image can be realized. Toward that end, there are notably two methodologies: one in relation to time, and one in relation to space. The former considers the experience of becoming a ball human in terms of time, while the latter considers the experience of becoming a ball human in terms of space. Therefore, the method that realizes the ball human image must give the appropriate weight to experience in time and experience in space.

THE THEORETICAL FOUNDATION AND GROUNDS FOR THE FORMATION OF THE BALL HUMAN METHODOLOGY

Before presenting the Methodology of the Ball Human, it is necessary to first make clear the reasons why it is possible to present such a methodology. In order to do this, we must look at the theoretical foundation and the grounds for the methodology. The theoretical foundation for the formation of the Methodology of the Ball Human relies on the Educational, Social, and Movement-Cultural Ontologies of the Ball Human and the Teleology of the Ball Human already presented. The grounds for the formation of this methodology is the fact that in scholastic physical education in every country around the world ball games are being practiced. The former is based on the development of the theory, while the latter comes from the practice of ball games.

THE CHARACTER OF THE METHODOLOGY OF THE BALL HUMAN

There are two characters associated with the content of the Methodology of the Ball Human. First, it is an unchangeable, universal, abstract methodology, applicable to any country at any time. Second, as countries and times change, it is a concrete, realistic methodology that changes accordingly. The Methodology of the Ball Human is constructed with the former at the core, while the latter surrounds it, both working together to preserve the relationship. More specifically, the former is the area of the methodology based on the common qualities of all countries and constructed by the physical education and sports researchers of every country in the world so that the practice of ball games in scholastic physical education in every country in the world serves to realize the ball human image. Meanwhile, the latter is the area of the methodology that has the quality that it grasps the differences in the realistic aspects of the ball human, i.e. country, time, age, sex, school, etc., as differences in realistic aspects.

ELEMENTS OF THE FORMATION OF THE CONTENTS OF THE METHODOLOGY OF THE BALL HUMAN

In regard to the formation of the Methodology of the Ball Human, both the theoretical foundation and the practical grounds have already been presented. However, I believe that the latter, the practical grounds, gives an extraordinarily important reason for the formation of the Methodology of the Ball Human. Namely, because of the existence of the purpose of the universal substance of the ball human, this points to the variable, concrete purpose of the ball human. The constitution of the teleology of the ball human relies on the support/being-supported relationship between these two sides, which is a relationship that acts dynamically and mutually to support each side. The ball human image of the former is the *purpose* of the ball human, while the ball human image of the latter is the *goal* of the ball human. The difference between these words clearly points to the difference between the universal purpose and practice of ball games in physical education programs, the existence of the practice of ball games in society, and because of the existence of physical education teachers, mentors, pupils and students who play a function in society, the need for the Methodology of the Ball Human becomes apparent.

In that case, physical education teachers and mentors are those who lead students to become ball humans and realize the ball human image, while students and followers who receive all forms of ball game education are those who look toward becoming all forms of ball humans and realizing all forms of the ball human image. Therefore, the human relationships of the teachers and mentors and students and followers in the phenomenon of the ball game will all become the ball human and realize the ball human image. It is a mutual relationship that exists to realize the ball human image.

Those fostering the ball human have experience in the past of fully becoming a ball human in order to realize the ball human image. They are those who possess the leadership qualifications to be able to realize the ball human image. On the other hand, those becoming ball humans must receive leadership in order to realize the ball human image. They are those of whom study ability is demanded.

Figure 10. Ball Human Image*

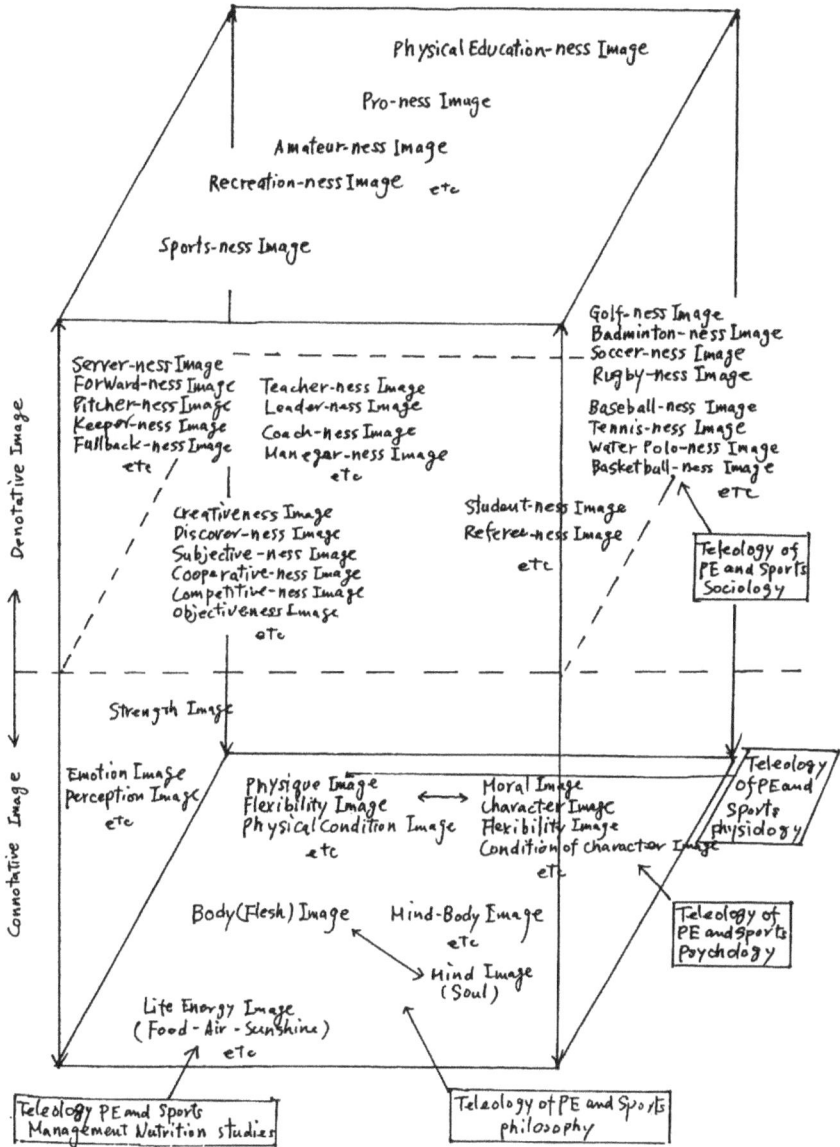

* In physical education and sports, the ball human forms the special society of the ball game. It works ideally in a unique way. At the same time, it is regulated in a unique way and exists ideally.

49

With the relationship between physical education teachers, who try to realize the ball human image and foster ball humans, and students, who study while looking toward becoming ball humans and realizing the ball human image, as the grounds, the various structural elements of the methodology of the various kinds of ball humans are formed. Specifically, these elements include study, leadership, evaluation, curriculum, educational resources, study ability, study processes, leadership ability, skill, etc. Classifying these elements into large groups, we may divide them into study, leadership, and educational resources. The terms "skill," "study ability," "study processes," etc. are all terms connected with the student or follower becoming a ball human and trying to realize the ball human image, and are therefore "study" terms. The terms "leadership ability," "evaluation," "curriculum," etc. are all terms connected with the teachers and mentors trying to realize the ball human image and turn their students into ball humans, and are therefore "leadership" terms. Finally, that which brings the leadership and study together at the place of the ball game are the educational resources. The structural elements of the Methodology of the Ball Human are systematized in the manner described in Figure 11.

Figure 11. The Structural Elements of the Methodology of the Ball Human

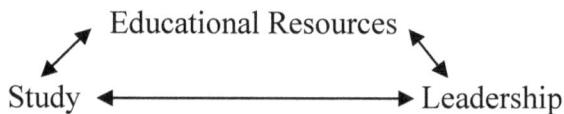

Study. This is the state of those becoming ball humans in which they learn all of the various things they must learn from those helping them to become ball humans in order to realize the ball human image. Also, we will call "students" those who, under the supervision of those fostering the ball human, strive to learn that which they need to become a ball human. Furthermore, "study ability" is ability that students possess to learn all the constructive knowledge required in order to become a ball human and realize the ball human image. "Skill" is a part of study ability, and is the condition of the mastery of the necessary techniques required to become a ball human and realize the ball human image. Also, "study process" is the process by which, under the leadership of those fostering the ball human, those becoming ball humans learn all of the relevant knowledge.

Leadership. This is defined as the leading of those who will become ball humans by those who will foster their becoming ball humans by giving them all the various knowledge they will need toward the goal of realizing the ball human image. "Leadership ability" is the ability of those fostering ball humans, with the goal of realizing the ball human image, to fully develop those becoming ball humans. The "leadership process" is the process by which those fostering ball humans, with the goal of realizing the ball human image, lead those becoming ball humans. Furthermore, "evaluation" is the process by which those fostering ball humans decide what level those becoming ball humans have reached and how far they have advanced in approaching the realization of the ball human image. "Curriculum" is the study route through which those fostering ball humans lead those becoming ball humans in order to realize the ball human image.

Educational Resources. We collectively use this term to refer to all materials those fostering ball humans use to lead those becoming ball humans to realize the ball human image along with all study materials used by those becoming ball humans aiming to realize the ball human image. Therefore, the educational resources play the role of inter-mediary in the formation of the leadership and study of the ball human, and are a necessary methodological element in the realization of the ball human image. The educational resources include natural educational resources and man-made educational resources. The former are sunshine, air, weather (clear, rain, snow, clouds), air pressure (wind), water (water in a pool), earth (ground), etc. The latter include gymnasium, lighting, racquet, bat, table tennis table, tennis net, handball goal, soccer goal, water polo goal, ice hockey goal, skating rink, pool, etc. Therefore, in the broad sense of the word, "educational resources" refers to the combination of natural educational resources and man-made natural resources, but when taken in the narrow sense of the word, refers mostly to man-made educational resources.

THE CONSTRUCTION METHOD OF THE METHODOLOGY OF THE BALL HUMAN

It is imperative that we use the terminology of the structural elements of the Methodology of the Ball Human, namely study (skill, study process, etc.), leadership (evaluation, curriculum, leadership process, leadership ability, etc.) and educational resources in order to realize the ball human image. However, it is also necessary to answer the question of how the content of these elements can be given substance. I will now present these kinds of problems related to the construction of the Methodology of the Ball Human.

From the standpoint of those dealing with fundamental theory of physical education studies, it is possible to construct a methodology that answers these kinds of questions. The Methodology of the Ball Human should use the original specialized vocabulary from each specialized area of physical education, and considering study, leadership, and educational resources, etc. we can create a separate methodology from each field of physical education that serves to realize every partial image of the ball human that emerges from that field. In regard to the Methodology of the Ball Human from physical education physiology, for instance, while considering study, leadership, and educational resources, we can construct an original methodology, using the specialized terms of physiology, such as strength, physique, health, and flexibility, that serves to realize the strength image, the physique image, the health image, and the flexibility image of the ball human.

Likewise, in regard to the Methodology of the Ball Human from physical education psychology, while considering study, leadership, and educational resources, we can construct an original methodology, using the specialized terms of psychology, such as character, morale, health, flexibility, etc., that serves to realize the character image, the morale image, the health image, and the flexibility image of the ball human. In regard to the Methodology of the Ball Human from physical education philosophy, while considering study, leadership, and

52

educational resources, we can construct an original methodology, using the specialized terms of philosophy, such as mind, body, the mind-body relationship, soul, flesh, etc., that serves to realize the mind image, the body image, the mind-body image, the soul image, and the flesh image of the ball human. In regard to the Methodology of the Ball Human from physical education educational science, while considering study, leadership, and educational resources, we can construct an original methodology, using the specialized terms of educational science, such as creativity, subjectivity, objectivity, cooperation, competition, etc., that serves to realize the creativity image, the subjectivity image, the objectivity image, the cooperation image, and the competition image of the ball human. In regard to the Methodology of the Ball Human from physical education sociology, while considering study, leadership, and educational resources, we can construct an original methodology, using the specialized terms of sociology, such as catcher, fullback, attacker, goalkeeper, amateur, recreation, etc., that serves to realize the catcher image, the fullback image, the goalkeeper Sage, the attacker image, the amateur image, and the recreation image of the ball human. In regard to the Methodology of the Ball Human from biomechanics, while considering study, leadership, and educational resources, we can construct an original methodology, using the specialized terms of biomechanics, such as grasp, throw, hit, catch, run, etc., that serves to realize the grasping image, the throwing image, the catching image, the hitting image, and the running image of the ball human. Moreover, the construction of the original methodologies of the ball human for each of these specialized fields of physical education must be living, changing entities, taking into account the realistic existence of things such as nationality, race, age, sex, etc., to be always the best methodology for physical education researchers of the present time. Therefore, research specialists in each field of physical education must, while referring to the knowledge in physical education history for advice, construct separate methodologies responsible for each specialized field.

In the above manner, it is possible to construct a Methodology of the Ball Human for every country in the world.

9

The Path Toward an Olympics in Which the Physical Education and Sports Studies Researchers of Each Country in the World Compete

Up to this point, the hypothesis has been presented, extracting the existential essence from the phenomenon of the ball game. In order to prove the hypothesis, the ontology was presented based on philosophical methods. In philosophical terms, this is *clear evidence*. In addition, from the ontology, the theory was developed further in both the teleology and the methodology, thereby furthering progress up the steps of formation of Ball Game Theory (world unified and different). With Ball Game Theory, which is simply a collective term for the theories concerning every type of ball game, we can go on to further the formation of scholarship in areas such as soccer studies, rugby studies, tennis studies, table tennis studies, golf studies, water polo studies, basketball studies, baseball studies, etc. In other words, this is a scholarship of practice (a theory) dealing with practice. This will be formed as theories of each type of ball game study dealing with the practice of each type of ball game.

This Ball Game Theory will appear as the fundamental theory for the purpose of constructing ball game studies in every country in the world. More specifically, it will be a theoretical system for constructing physical education and sports studies in every country in the world. With regard to the differences of history, thought, culture, etc., that exist between countries, this will be a theory that will be applicable to every country in which all types of ball games are practiced in physical education and in sports. In addition, it will also be applicable to the practice of ball games in the Olympics held by the IOC. This Ball Game Theory will deal with the whole theories of ball game studies, while also dealing with the partial theories from every field of physical education and sports studies, namely physical education and sports philosophy, physical education and sports psychology, physical education and sports physiology, physical education and sports sociology, etc. While consulting the facts in physical education and sports history and using the specialized terminology of every field, it will elucidate the realistic phenomenon of each type of ball game through experiment, surveys, and data. It will be able to confirm the scholarship as necessary to unify, from each specialized field, the ontologies, teleologies, and methodologies of all types of ball humans in every country in the world, in every era. At the same time, these partial theories will fit into the entire theory, namely Ball Game Theory, and promote the establishment of scholarship in soccer studies, rugby studies, tennis studies, etc. With the completion of this theory, the question "Why all types of ball games are being conducted by the educational ministries in scholastic physical education in every country in the world?" will be answered to general society from the standpoint of physical education and sports researchers. This means that the theory will carry a social responsibility to the practice of ball games in every country. Also, the theory will be able to answer the question "Why are social sports groups in every country and international sports groups (i.e. the IOC's Olympics) conducting all types of ball games?" from the standpoint of the world's physical education and sports researchers. Therefore, the various specialized research in physical education and sports studies based on the Ball Game Theory will be important social and nationalistic research that will have impact on the peaceful unification of differences between all nations. Thus, to those who achieve success with partial theories, it will be possible to award a physical education and sports studies doctorate (national doctorate) degree. Furthermore, the grounds and theoretical basis for the worthiness of these partial theories of the doctorate degree can be explained to general society and guaranteed through the Ball Game Theory. In other words, the doctorate degree in physical education and sports studies will gain social and international trust when evaluated as being objectively responsible, both within the country and without. The physical education and sports studies doctorate, which can be explained by the Ball Game Theory, will be registered with the education ministry in each country as a mark of achievement of physical education and sports research. This type of doctorate is a national doctorate, but at the World Academy for Physical Education and Sports Studies, which we will establish in the future, world doctorates will be chosen from the physical education and sports doctorates in every country. These people will take the leadership of world physical education and sports studies for us. In that case, of course, a very strict reviewing process will be required.

The standards and principles of this Ball Game Theory must be defended to the slightest degree by physical education and sports researchers of the world in order to preserve the health of physical education and sports studies in every country in the world. A Ball Game Studies Theory should be constructed which conforms to realistic society, reflects the factual uniqueness of every country in the world in society, culture, history, and thought, and can be socially responsible to the present practice of ball games. The nature of this job will most certainly become a national enterprise. Through this Ball Game Theory, we will clearly grasp each country in the world's differences as each country in the world and each country in the world's common points as each country in the world. We will form a harmonious whole in Ball Game Theory from these mutually different factors, and we will be able to see ball game studies of humanity. From the existence of the ball human, which is in one reality a human, we can go on to answer the age-old philosopher's question: What is a human?"

Just as there are rules common throughout the world in the practice of physical education and sports, there are rules common throughout the world relating to the method of research in the fields of physical education and sports theoretical research. These rules common throughout the world for physical education and sports research are embodied in the International Ball Games Studies for the Achievement of Peace.

Concerning the state of physical education and sports research today, there seem to be no rules about the way in which research is conducted. There is research without an objective, and irresponsible physical education methodologies and teleologies are appearing. In the carefree playing with words in every language among physical education and sports researchers there is no life, and it results in the

56

repetition of adult-like technical phrases. The purpose of this type of research becomes the experiments and insights themselves. Furthermore, physical education science researchers are aiming to acquire doctorate degrees in other fields. This is a contaminated situation that is far removed from the state of research for the sake of peace that I have put forth in this paper. I believe that, as true physical education and sports researchers, it is our responsibility to restore quickly the state of healthy research in physical education and sports studies. This paper, the "Theory of International Physical Education and Sports Studies for the Achievement of Peace," is an attempt to solve the most important problems toward that end. With it, we can solve all of the various problems related to ball games.

The evaluation and value judgments of physical education and sports research based on truth, as put forth. In this "Theory of International Physical Education and Sports Studies: for the Achievement of Peace," will take place today at, the universities in every country in the world, where doctorate degrees will be awarded by professors. In the future however, we, the physical education and sports researchers of the world, will establish a physical education and sports academy in every country and a world physical education and sports academy at which research will be publicly evaluated and doctorate degrees will be awarded. The awarding of the physical education and sports doctorate degree will not be limited to universities, but instead we must give all physical education and sports researchers an equal opportunity to receive the doctorate degree. The reason for this is that we physical education and sports researchers are basically people whose social function is to guarantee the practice of physical education and sports. We are not medical researchers or educational researchers. It is natural that when the title of an area of scholarship is unique, the content of that scholarship is unique as well. We believe that it is necessary to have truly superior, healthy physical education and sports researchers from every country in the world. In addition, we hope that in the future the physical education and sports researchers of every country in the world will adopt new attitudes. Instead of physical education and sports researchers performing physical education and sports research for the *sole purpose* of receiving the physical education and sports doctorate, we would like physical education and sports researchers to participate in physical education and sports research with a *true purpose,* that is, one associated with the achievement of peace. The purpose of every physical education and sports researcher, through the research in his or her specialized field, will be to contribute to peace. Based on the method of this research, the physical education and sports academies of every country will award the physical education and sports doctorate degree. I would like to reiterate emphatically that we physical education and sports researchers have one true purpose: *the realization* of *peace.* Why must the purpose of physical education and sports studies be peace? This is because peace gives birth to the production of the nation and mankind. This conclusion comes from the wisdom that without peace, the development of mankind would be unthinkable. Also, doctorates from every field of physical education and sports studies alike, including physical education and sports history, physical education and sports psychology, physical education and sports physiology, physical education and sports philosophy, physical education and sports sociology, must be given to society. If some field of physical education and sports research has a relatively high number of doctorates, it may give rise to a one-sided, deformed, unhealthy state of physical education and sports theory in all countries.

Among the doctorates that we see today, there are some abnormal, sick people, whose field of vision is narrow. When we present the physical education and sports doctorate to the world in the future, we have a social responsibility. It is necessary to describe the kind of person that we would like to have as physical education and sports doctorates:

- The physical education and sports doctorates are gentlemen and ladies. In other words, they must embody a harmony of abundant emotion and abundant wisdom. They must also be healthy people that exhibit behavioral conduct based on the perception that they are human.

- The physical education and sports doctorate will have a social responsibility to the practice of physical education and sports. He or she will advance theories and support the educational ministries of all countries and all sports groups.

- The individual physical education and sports doctorate will love the country in which he was born and he will be a person who encourages others to love the countries in which they were born.

- The physical education and sports doctorate will be a person that contributes to peace in every country and to world peace through research in each specialized field.

10

The Establishment of a World Academy for Physical Education and Sports Studies and a Physical Education and Sports Studies Academy in Every Country

It has become evident that, from now on, we physical education and sports researchers must progressively advance from our previous era of dependence to an era of independence; from a childlike era to an adult-like era; from an era of learning to an era of teaching; from an era of chaos to an era of order. Likewise, in order to insure that physical education and sports studies will be a study of peace, we physical education and sports researchers must now become independent from the scholarship we have relied on in the past, such as educational studies, medicine, etc.; we must become independent from the educational ministries of every country in the world; and we must become independent of all physical education sports groups. Thus, we will support, through theory, national education ministries, social sports groups and other organizations, relying on the completion of my physical education and sports theory and on the World Physical Education and Sports Academy and the physical education and sports academies in each country that will have peace as their purpose. On the other hand, I believe we must create an effective working relationship with other areas of scholarship, such as education- al studies, medicine, literature, etc. Also, the physical education and sports researchers of every country have a social responsibility to the practice of physical education and sports, and they must work to guarantee the development of support for peace in every country and for world peace.

This Ball Game Theory is a necessary theory that must be put forth for the future establishment of the World Physical Education and

Sports Academy in New York. Thus, we must learn from the physical education and sports researchers in America about all types of the ball human in America, from the physical education and sports researchers in the Soviet Union about all types of the ball human in the Soviet Union, from the physical education and sports researchers in China about all types of the ball human in China, from the physical education and sports researchers in France about all types of the ball human in France, from the physical education and sports researchers in Japan about all types of the ball human in Japan, from the physical education and sports researchers in Sweden about all types of the ball human in Sweden-from the physical education and sports researchers in all other countries about all types of the ball human in those countries. I would like to see the world doctorate degree in physical education and sports studies be an academic degree with authority, given to physical education and sports researchers who have contributed to peace (as determined by a strict examination by the World Physical Education and Sports Academy) in a *competitive* format. The world doctorates will be selected from the national doctorates in each country, but they must be able to lead physical education and sports studies research in every country in the world through their respective specialized fields. They must be guarantors, through true leadership, who encourage the development of support for the peace of mankind from the fields of physical education and sports studies.

I would like to declare here, with the establishment of this Ball Game Theory, to the physical education and sports researchers of the world, that the purpose of physical education and sports research is a purpose of national peace and world peace. Thus, I would like the physical education and sports researchers of every country to, using this Ball Game Theory as the foundation for physical education and sports research, bring this theory back to their own countries, construct a theory of ball game studies for their own countries, preserve the social existence of the educational ministry and physical education and sports groups in their own countries, and work toward the develop-ment of support for peace in their own countries. Also, through this work, I would like them to nurture the independence of history, tradition, culture, etc., in their own countries. The reason for this is that the true path to world peace begins with the effort toward realization of peace in one's own country.

Physical education and sports researchers must return to the path by which Baron de Coubertin founded the modern Olympic games. Physical education and sports practice toward peace must begin in the form of physical education and sports theory. The peaceful path that we, the physical education and sports researchers, must try to walk in the future is a natural path that is illuminated by facts from history. We must follow this natural path-the path of physical education and sports fad. I would like to request that, through research concerning ball game studies, the physical education and sports researchers of the world be responsible to the goal of peace and have pride in the goal of peace. In the future, we will conduct representative research presentations of ball game studies research from every country in the world at the World Physical Education and Sports Academy. We will foster the growth of world authorities. Thus, from these world authorities, we can expect a guarantee of peace in the countries of the human. From here, I am working diligently toward the establishment of the World Physical Education and Sports Academy in New York City. This is for the benefit of the physical education and sports researchers of the world, and for the benefit of world peace.

11

A Final Word

This "Theory of International Ball Game Studies for the Achievement of Peace" is a theory that functions as one part of physical education and sports studies, however other studies, such as track and field studies, swimming studies, dance studies, martial arts studies, gymnastics studies, skiing studies, skating studies, etc., remain. Therefore, I call upon the physical education and sports researchers of the world to pick up their pens in order to confirm these areas of scholarship and publish their written work. At the same time, while I have already presented the social role of physical education and sports researchers, in order to fully realize this in the future, we must request assistance from the educational ministries of all countries of the world, companies that produce and publish literature about physical education and sports, companies that produce and sell sports merchandise, organizations practicing physical education and sports in every country in the world (i.e., the IOC), and organizations functioning to promote the development of world peace, such as the United Nations and the Nobel Organization, etc. The reason for this is that we, the physical education and sports researchers of the world, have a social, national, and human responsibility to lead the children of the future to the importance of peace through peaceful practice and integration of theories in the world's physical education and sports classrooms and in physical education and sports groups. We, the physical education and sports researchers, in looking toward peace, the highest goal of mankind, must strive toward independence from all other areas of scholarship. From there, we, the physical education and sports researchers, will be able to take on the social responsibility of working toward peace for mankind and peace in every country. This is the only true path for our physical education and sports research.

Part II

Theory of International Track and Field Studies for the Achievement of Peace

1

A Word from the Author

The term *track and field human* is a symbolic term that works toward national peace and world peace. We, the world's physical education and sports scholars, must treat this word as dearly as our own lives. This is because without the existence of the track and field human, none of the language concerning track and field and research concerning track and field could be formed. The existence builds and determines it all. The term "track and field human" is the universal language of the world's physical education and sports scholars. It is a specialized term, even a holy term.

I present this paper for the benefit of all the physical education and sports scholars of each of the world's nations alike.

2

Establishing the Hypothesis for Creating Track and Field Studies

What is physical education and sports studies? I have been struggling with this difficult question for a long time. I have read various philosophical writings on the subject, and have spent much time contemplating them. As a result, it was about seven or eight years ago that I first reached the design of a vague answer to this question. As I am writing this thesis now, the overall concept has become entirely clear. I now believe that the key to answering this question truly lies in the practice itself of physical education and sports. I believe that the fact to which perception points is the true teacher.

Next, I would like to proceed in my writing to affirm track and field studies. However, for this task there is an order of theoretical development. First, we must grasp the structure of the phenomenon of track and field through perceptive intuition and extract its existential essence. Then, in order to answer the question "What is the phenomenon of track and field competition?" I will derive my hypothesis. In order to test whether the hypothesis is true or false, I will apply it to the factual phenomenon of track and field and see whether or not it can explain the phenomenon. Then, if I prove the hypothesis, I can put forth a teleology and a methodology as a grounds for the proof. Through this chain of processes, I believe that the scholarship of track and field studies can be widely established. Following this order, I will proceed to develop the theory.

Moreover, in the course of advancing the theory, or perhaps in the course of building the theory, new words such as *track and field human, track and field human image, marathon human, short-distance human, running long jump human,* etc., will be introduced. These are the key words of this theory. I have thought up these words in order to facilitate the formation of the theory.

I will be attempting to affirm track and field studies as a part of physical education and sports studies. However, in order to do this I must present the important factors in the make-up of the phenomenon of track and field and the relationship between them. Therefore, I have tried to explain the basis of the establishment of the track and field phenomenon in the following figure (see Figure 12).

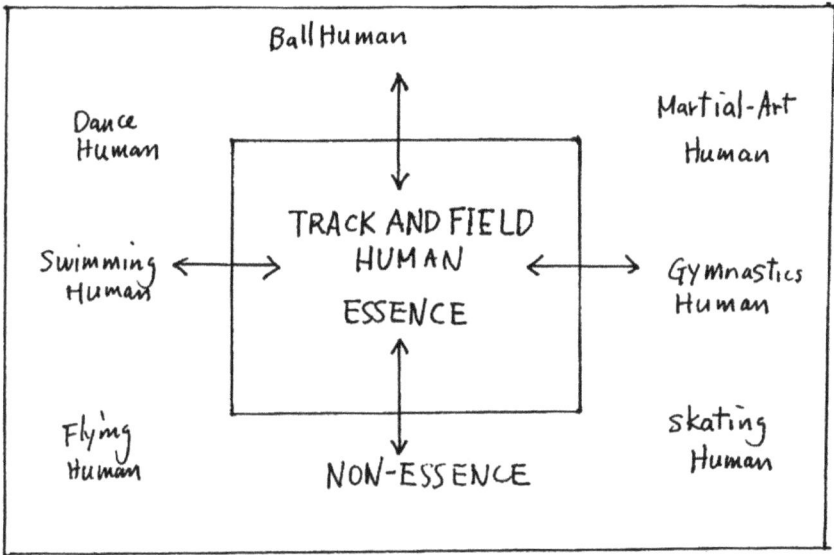

Figure 12. The Formation actors of the Living Phenomenon of the Track and Field Human

Incidentally, in order to explain the phenomenon, I have presented words here such as track and field human, skiing human, skating human, swimming human, etc. This is language that directly points to the fact that each human is a human in reality. For instance, the phrase *track and field human* is a phrase that points directly to the aspects of two sides acting together in a dynamic, living relationship-the human and the ground. These actions include the intentions of running, walking, jumping, throwing, etc. The ground itself is alive, as when it flies in the air as dirt. As for the human, the human feels emotion and reacts by saying things like "I won!" "I did it!" or "I lost!" There are many other things that are said in the heat of the moment.

Now, based on the figure above, we will go on to explain the basis for the formation of the lively phenomenon of track and field competition. The essence of the phenomenon of track and field is the track and field human as presented in the figure. It is the basis of special properties associated with track and field competition, namely the track and field human. Specifically, the elements acting in the phenomenon of track and field competition are the track and field human. *Track and field human* points to the aspects of the human and the ground acting together in the phenomenon of track and field.

Also, in these situations, the ground can be a man-made road consisting of concrete or asphalt, or natural mound, such as a mountain path, a snow trail, or a gravel road. There is also the man-made all-weather ground. We will collectively use the term "ground" to refer to all surfaces, whether man-made or natural, that are designed for the practice of track and field competition. As for the human, there are different kinds of sex, male and female. From the perspective of nationality, there are Americans, Chinese, French, Japanese, Canadians, Soviets, etc. From the perspective of race, there are blacks, whites, yellows, etc. Also, looking at the human's age, there are 10-year-olds, 20-year-olds, 35-year-olds, etc.

From the facts presented above, I will present the following hypothesis concerning the phenomenon of track and field competition. Namely, the existential essence of track and field competition is the track and field human. **When practicing track and field competition, the human does not become a human, the human becomes a track and field human.** *In other words, the phenomenon of track and field competition is the conduct of becoming a track and field human and is conduct for the purpose of becoming a track and field human.*

I will attempt to prove this hypothesis by looking at the living phenomenon of every type of track and field competition, and relying on the philosophical method of perceptive insight. However, in that case, this is not a scientific method. This is a proof by the actual existence of the track and field human in every country in the world. Therefore, instead of using the word "proof," I shall use the word "evidence." So using the term "track and field human," I will look at the living phenomenon of track and field competition in detail, and I will explain it systematically. The format of this evidence will of the Track and Field Human (system of existence). First, I will present the

70

social existence of the track and field human, and I will show evidence for the living existence of the track and field human in every country in the world in the expression of every country in the world.

3

Proof 1-The Social Ontology of the Track and Field Human

The social existence of the track and field human is divided into a connotative structure and a denotative structure. While these work together dynamically, they appear as the special, social existence of the concrete track and field human.

THE CONNOTATIVE STRUCTURE

The connotative structure of the track and field human itself generates the denotative structure, an area that is fundamentally attached to its own social existence. The connotative structure of the track and field human itself regulates the denotative structure while at the same time it is regulated by the denotative structure. It is in this relationship, not with uniquely connotative actions, that the realistic existence is based. The basis of the denotative structure of the track and field human and its lively, variable, dynamic aspects are in the function of the connotative structure of the track and field human. Therefore, this is the reason for the expression of a unique denotative structure of the track and field human.

There are various types of connotative actions of the track and field human. There are all of the visual perceptions, walking, running, jumping, throwing (all actions of the movement human side), and making one walk, making one run, making one throw, making one jump (all actions of the ground side). The existence of the track and field human appears from these actions of walking, throwing, jumping, and running. Furthermore, if we attempt to analyze the track and field human's action types of running, throwing, walking, and jumping, we see that they are formed by the actions of pushing, kicking, and hitting in the relationship between the movement human and the ground. This relationship is one of pushing and being pushed, kicking and being kicked, hitting and being hit, etc. Thus, these various elements act to establish the actions of running, walking, jumping, and throwing.

The types of actions of the track and field human, running, walking, jumping and throwing, are composed of skilled actions and life actions, and they appear in the way of existence of the track and field human. We will look at the realistic existence of the track and field human, and, using the specialized terminology from every specialized field, we will explore and clearly explain these actions. For this purpose, we can use the analytical chart in the figure below (See Figure 13).

Once we have done this, we see that the life actions, the origin of the life of the track and field human, make the formation of the connotative structure possible. Thus, the formation of the philo-sophical terms "mind," "soul," "mind-body," and "flesh," are based on these life actions. Using this specialized terminology of philosophy, physical education, and sports philosophers can bring to light the components of these actions of the track and field human. Further-more, we can look at the track and field human from points of view other than the actions of mind and body. For instance, the components of the actions of the track and field human can be examined using the terminology of physiology, such as "body strength," "physique," "flexibility," "health," etc., or the terms of psychology, such as "morale," "flexibility," "character," "mental health," etc. The former is the domain of physical education and sports physiologists, while the latter is the research domain of physical education and sports psychologists. Also, if we look at the realistic existence of the track and field human and use the terminology of movement studies, such as "pushing," "hitting," "running," "walking," "jumping," "throwing," etc., the connotative structure of the track and field human can be clearly examined. This is the domain of physical education and sports movement studies.

Therefore, these various elements that form the connotative structure of the track and field human live and act in a unique way, and they act in unison with the realistic existence of the track and field human appearing as an entire, acting track and field human. In other words, the track and field human is the basis for the specialized terminology from all the appear as a many-sided, dynamic unity the

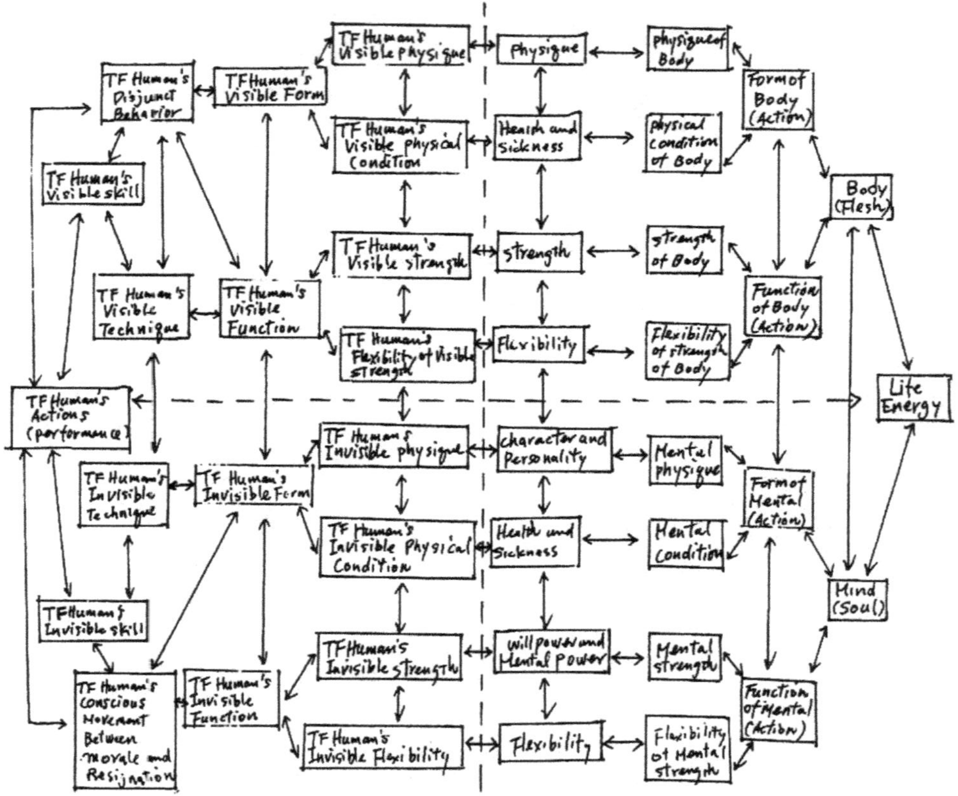

Figure 13. (Track and Field Human Skilled Action Types) ←→ (Track and Field Human Life Energy Types)

weight, depth, livelihood, and breadth of the language from each field are things that refer to each specialized field.

These actions of the connotative structure of the track and field human act at the same time to form the denotative structure.

THE DENOTATIVE STRUCTURE

There are various elements that constitute the social aspects of the track and field human. Also, these various elements are unique social actions that are dynamic, variable, and alive. As for the various elements that form the social aspects of the track and field human, we can see them in the figure below (See Figure 14).

Figure 14. The Social Aspects of the Track and Field Human

	First Analysis	Second Analysis
The Denotative Structure as the Social Existence of the Track and Field Human	Partial Expression of Social Phenomenon of the Track and Field Human	Sports-nesss Physical Ed.-ness Recreation-ness/ Competitiveness
	Partial Expression of Social Phenomenon of the Track and Field Human	Combativeness/ Cooperativeness Primitiveness/ Modernity

Sports-ness–Physical Education-ness

There are situations in which the aspects of track and field appear in the educational content and in practice in schools and corresponding locations where there is an educational environment. This is the aspect of the phenomenon of the track and field human in scholastic physical education. The physical education-ness of the track and field human is the place of educational negotiation between the physical education teachers and students. As opposed to the sports-ness of the track and field human, the scale of this phenomenon is smaller and its scope is limited. On the other hand, there is the phenomenon of the track and field human that is practiced by general society. This is the expression of the sports-ness of the track and field human. It is formed by the sum total of leaders and those being led. If we compare the sports-ness of the track and field human to the physical education-ness of the track and field human, it has the property that it spans a wide scope, without distinctions of sex, age, occupation, etc. In this way, the sports-ness and the physical education-ness of the track and field human serve as the basis for the existence of the formation elements of the social aspects of the track and field human. Therefore, based on the phenomenon of track and field, we establish the terms sports-ness and physical education-ness.

Recreation-ness and Competitiveness

In the phenomenon of track and field, there are situations in which all types of track and field events are practiced, by a group of employees or by a group of some other relationship, for health purposes, to restore body strength, or to improve human relationships. This is the recreation-ness of the track and field human. Its property is that there is always an atmosphere of harmony in which hearts and souls can come into contact. On the other hand, in the phenomenon of track and field there are also meets, etc., in which the competitive abilities in track and field compete with each other. This is the competitiveness of the track and field human. While obeying the rules of track and field competition, each acts to beat its opponents, and a unique atmosphere of tension is created. The greater the scale of the track and field meet, the more conspicuous the competitiveness of the track and field human appears. For example, in phenomena such as international track and field meets and track and field meets in the Olympics, the competitiveness of the track and field human is clearly evident. In this and field human forms the phenomenon of track appears through the social aspects of recreation-ness and competitiveness. Furthermore, in the competitiveness of the track and field human, we can see the social aspects of amateur-ness and professional-ness as well.

Combativeness-Cooperativeness

In the social aspects of the track and field human, we find combativeness and cooperation. In the various types of relays and point-based events in the phenomena of track and field meets, based on school rivalries, regional rivalries, or national rivalries, we find the expression of the cooperativeness of the track and field human. In the instant when the track and field human hands off the relay baton, the individual and some other create a team consciousness. On the other hand, we can also find the condition when, based on the criteria of track and field competition, the space between ball humans is filled with a mutual harshness, and each tries to compete with the other. This is the expression of the combativeness of the track and field human. Furthermore, the combativeness of the track and field human is not limited to just combativeness against another individual or another team. We also see combativeness of the individual against himself. In this way, the combativeness and cooperativeness of the track and field human are elements that form the social existence of the track and field human. Therefore, we can establish and use the terms combat and cooperation.

Primitiveness and Modernity

In the phenomenon of track and field competition, there is often direct contact between the human and the ground. This is an expression of the primitiveness of the track and field human. For example, in the Olympics of Ancient Greece, there were those who ran barefooted, coming into direct contact with the ground. Also, in modern times in the phenomenon of the marathon, there are still some runners who run barefooted, acting directly on the ground. On the other hand, in the phenomenon of track and field competition there are track and field humans that use all kinds of spikes, sports shoes, etc., for the interaction between the human and the ground. These are used when there is a relationship to the ground in the actions of running, jumping, etc. There is indirect action on the ground in short-distance running with special-purpose, short-distance running spikes, in middle-distance running with special-purpose, middle-distance running spikes, in hurling with special-purpose hurler's shoes, and in mountain climbing with special-purpose, mountain-climber's boots. Also, some of the types of ground on which the track and field human acts consist of man-made materials. For example, the track and field human performs the actions of running, walking, etc. on surfaces such as asphalt and concrete. These are all expressions of the modernity of the track and field human. As we move away from the natural contact between human and ground in the phenomenon of track and field competition, and as the method of contact becomes more indirect and more man-made, the track and field human itself becomes more man-made and is removed from the nature of the original track and field human. In the above manner, the primitiveness and the modernity are the elements of the factors that form the social existence of the track and field human. Therefore, we are obligated to use these words in track and field studies.

SUMMARY

The track and field human described here appears in social aspects in every country in the world. Furthermore, in every country of the world, there is the phenomenon of the social expression of the unique track and field human to each country. In China as Chinese, in the Soviet Union as Soviets, in America as Americans, and in Japan as Japanese, the track and field human exists possessing these special qualities. Also, there are several things we can name that act in direct relation to the formation of the social existence of this track and field human. For example, the actions of weight and gravity, the actions of weather, wind, and lightning, and the actions of the special equipment used in track and field competition, etc. We can divide these into man-made actions and the actions of nature, but they are all acting in relation to the social existence of the track and field human. At the same time, however, they are all a harmonious whole, acting in the formation of the social existence of the track and field human.

In the manner above, using the language "track and field human," it has become possible to explain the living phenomenon of track and field competition as a living phenomenon. In other words, we can show clear evidence for the formation of the phenomenon of a special, concrete human, called the "track and field human," by the phenomenon of track and field competition. Thus, the social ontology of the track and field human, the first proof of the previously noted hypothesis is now complete. The existential essence of track and field competition is the track and field human, which directly refers to the existence of the unifying, dynamic actions of the ground and the human. Meanwhile, I have confirmed the phenomenon of the social existence of the track and field human in track and field competition in every country in the world.

4

Proof 2–The Educational Ontology of the Track and Field Human

The track and field human also exists in educational aspects in every country in the world, primarily in schools. This educational existence of the track and field human comes from a connotative structure and a denotative structure. While these two act together, they exist in general society with certain special aspects.

THE CONNOTATIVE STRUCTURE

In the actions concerned with the action of the track and field human, there are those actions that rely on the skill of track and field competition ingrained in the individual, and those for which this is not the case. The former are the skilled actions of the track and field human, while the latter are the simple actions of the track and field human.

Let us try to gain some insight into the latter, the simple actions of the track and field human. These actions of the track and field human can be explained in other words as the behavior and conduct of the track and field human.

The phenomenon of track and field competition is the phenomenon that forms the dynamic development of the human and the ground. Therefore, based on the phenomenon of track and field competition, namely the separation-contact behavior of the ground and the human, we can understand all of the actions of the track and field human. Meanwhile, the human in track and field competition, through the actions of the unconscious-conscious makes the phenomenon of the living, breathing, moving ground more apparent. This consciousness encourages the formation of the conscious phenomenon of resignation. On the other hand, the ground in track and field competition waits for the actions of the human, and it acts to support the actions of the human. For example, through the actions of the ground, which can appear as sound, a cloud of sand, or flying dirt and mud, we can confirm these extroverted actions in these aspects of the ground.

Therefore, the human and the ground in track and field competition appear in a special existence in which they mutually seek each other and are sought by one another. Thus, both mutually act together to form the special phenomenon of track and field competition. The action of morale/resignation of the track and field human that occurs there provides a continuity in time and a positiveness in space.

With this said, let us now attempt to collect all of the language that explains the actions of the track and field human. Generally speaking, this language can be divided into words explaining the human side of track and field competition and words explaining the ground side of track and field competition.

Of the former, we can find words such as run, walk, make contact, separate, push, dash, spot, trip, fall down, stagger, lie down, jump, rise, throw, revolve, etc. Also, there are also words explaining the ground side of track and field competition which are words referring to the various actions of the ground, such as line, goal, 100 meters, 400 meters, 1,500 meters, 110 miles per hour, foul, fair, fall, stick, rise, one more lap, etc.

If we use these words to explain the phenomenon of track and field in a sentence, then we can say that:

"some track and field human performed the action
of *running* for *100 meters*"

(human side) (ground side)

    Or

"some track and field human performed the action
of *throwing* a discus *40 meters*"

(human side)   (ground side)

In this manner, when we express in a sentence the acting content of the track and field human in the phenomenon of track and field competition, the existence of the human and the ground is always included. Furthermore, even in the statistics kept for records, the existence of both sides is always included.

If we arrange these actions of the connotative structure of the track and field human, we can summarize them in the following chart (See Figure 15).

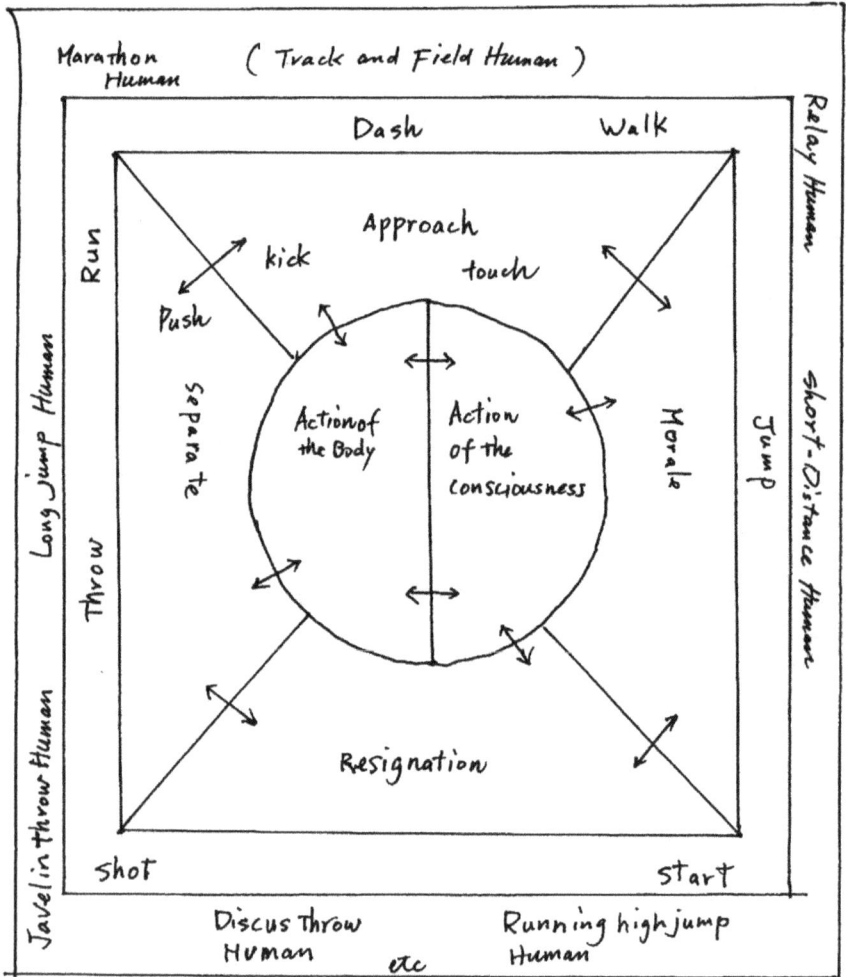

Figure 15.

Specifically, the action that is the center of the actions of the connotative structure is the joint action of the separation/contact of the human and the ground (action of the body) and the action of the consciousness (which exists at the time of the action of separation/ contact) of morale/resignation. As for words that explain both the separation/contact and morale/resignation actions, there are several, including push, kick, make contact, etc. These actions of the track and field human act as the central part of the connotative structure. Then, around these, the words are born that affirm the part that includes the actions of running, walking, jumping, starting, throwing, etc. Thus, the formation of these words brings about the formation of each kind of track and field human within the track and field human, including the marathon human, the pole vault human, the running high jump human, the short-distance human, etc.

The connotative structure of the educational existence of the track and field human is formed in the manner above, and it exists in every country in the world. At the same time, these actions of the connotative structure act to form the denotative structure as well.

THE DENOTATIVE STRUCTURE

The track and field human exists in scholastic physical education. In other words, we can say that the track and field human appears possessing educational aspects. In that case, we can enumerate the various special qualities at work in the educational aspects within the track and field human.

Sociality

The track and field human appears in special social aspects within education. The basic human relationship that forms these is that between teacher and student. There is also a certain uniqueness in the relationship between students as the relationship between track and field humans. Both sides compete while mutually recognizing the existence of the other, and using the special rules, equipment, facilities, etc., of track and field competition, they form a unique society.

Discovery-ness

If we consider each type of event in track and field competition in other terms, they are really invented products of the formation of the existence of the track and field human. These products are cultural treasures that serve to enrich the lives of the average human. Furthermore, these events in track and field competition (which were discovered) have improved with the passing of time before they reach us today. The discovery of events in track and field competition enlarges the number of events in track and field and enlarges the existence of different types of track and field human. Likewise, it provides variability in the aspects of the track and field human.

Cooperativeness

In the phenomenon of track and field competition, there are cases in which the track and field human exhibits aspects of cooperativeness in which it works together with another. The cooperativeness of the track and field human appears in relay races, relay marathons, etc., when, although there are differences between oneself and others, these differences of skill level, sex, etc., are overcome. Each type of track and field human (and each individual who looks on indirectly and is supported) forms the aspect of cooperativeness seen in the track and field human. This cooperativeness of the track and field human is the unique aspect of cooperation within the society of track and field competition.

Creativity

There are situations in which the track and field human, in the dynamic space of track and field competition, acts in a manner that promotes creativity. The creativity of the track and field human enhances interest in all track and field events and deepens the track and field human. The creativity of the track and field human ensures the flourishing of every type of track and field competition and encourages the development of track and field events. "In what way should I act with my body so that I can jump faster, farther, and higher?" The solution to this kind of question lies in the effort and creativity of the individual.

In the manner above, the educational existence of the track and field human functions as a living, two-fold structure of connotation and denotation. These function together to act in a unique way. Finally, in every country in the world, every type of the track and field human exists educationally in the expression of every country in the world forming the world of track and field competition.

5

Proof 3–The Movement-Cultural Ontology of the Track and Field Human

The track and field human as a movement human ingrains movement culture into himself, and exists possessing a movement-cultural side. This comes about from a connotative structure and a denotative structure that act together to maintain its unique function and that live and exist as a whole.

THE CONNOTATIVE STRUCTURE

The track and field human as a movement human itself is a human that is organically constructed with a head, torso, hands, feet, etc. Internally, the human is composed of muscles, bones, organs, a brain, etc., which all depend on blood. Meanwhile, the track and field human as the ground is all of the land on the Earth, which can be divided into all-weather ground, indoor ground, sand paths, paved roads, dirt roads, mountain paths, grass paths, etc. We can, of course, make a general distinction in this group between man-made grounds and those natural grounds in whose creation humans played no part. These various grounds are grounds for the purpose of running, for the purpose of walking, for the purpose of kicking, for the purpose of throwing, and for the purpose of jumping. They are grounds that always maintain a relationship with the human in the world of track and field competition. They all ad either as the skilled actions or behavioral conduct actions of a group or of an individual, based on the actions of nature, such as weight, gravity, temperature, weather, air pressure, etc., and based on the various kinds of man-made actions, such as physical education teachers, grandstands, lighting, equipment (blocks, hurdles, etc.). However, these actions are joined with the substance of the actions of perception, thought, emotion, etc., which are based on the living body of the track and field human as a movement human. Therefore, the track and field human as a movement human appears as a complex set of the actions of each individual.

As the actions of the individual, both sides, the track and field human as a movement human and the track and field human as the movement ground (or to use a different expression, the living ground and the enlivened ground) mutually provide aspects of approach, contact and separation. These actions are composed of various types of actions, including contacting, pushing, kicking, etc.

As the actions of the group, both sides, the track and field human of the group as a movement human and the track and field human as the ground of the group mutually provide aspects of approach, contact and separation. These actions are composed of various types of actions, including yelling between friendly teammates, signs, and gestures.

Also, the skilled actions of the individual or the group are based on the actions of the eyes, ears, tongue, and nose of the acting track and field human as a movement human, the actions of its internal organs such as the stomach and the intestines, the actions of the brain, such as the actions of the cerebrum and the mid-brain (i.e., external perceptions of sight, hearing, taste, touch, smell, etc., and the internal perceptions that come from the organs, bones, muscles, etc.), and the actions of thought and emotion. Thus in the form of "perception/thought/emotion," the human dynamically participates in the actions as skill in an independent and dependent relation- ship. For example:

> Just a little bit more–Hang in there!
> The ground is soft–It's hard to run.
> The ground is hot–My legs are burning!
> Etcetera.

All of these point to the condition of the living actions of perception/thought/emotion of the track and field human.

THE DENOTATIVE STRUCTURE

The track and field human as a movement human appears in the following kinds of movement-cultural aspects in forming the special world of track and field competition.

Running High Jump-ness (the running high jump human)

The running high jump human as a movement human is a special human inherent in the track and field human. The running high jump human exists in reality in association with the equipment (bar, stand, soft mat, sandbox, etc.), facilities, terminology, clothing, etc., that form the world of the running high jump. The characteristic of the actions of the running high jump human is that it acts to try to rise against gravity.

Javelin Throw-ness (the javelin throw human)

The javelin throw human as a movement human is a special human inherent in the track and field human. In the world of the javelin throw, there are unique rules, equipment, terminology, clothing, etc. These form the special world of the javelin throw human.

Short Distance-ness (the short distance human)

Among the types of track and field human, there is the short-distance human. The short-distance human forms the world of short distance, and using special equipment, clothing, terminology (such as "dash," "elongated start," etc.), facilities, etc., it appears as the short-distance human. Among the short- distance humans, there are the 100 meter human, the 200 meter human, the 400 meter human, etc. Each exists as its own human forming its own world.

Marathon-ness (the marathon human)

Among the types of track and field human, there is the marathon human. This creates the unique world of the marathon. In the world of the marathon, unique terminology, equipment, facilities, etc., are used, serving to establish the existence of the marathon human. The marathon human draws many onlookers to its route, thus forming the world of the marathon.

Relay-ness (the relay human)

Among the types of the track and field human, there is the relay human. The relay human forms the society of the relay, thus forming a unique world. At present, among the types of the relay human are the 400 meter relay human, the 1,600 meter relay human, and the long-distance relay human. In the society of the relay human, there is unique terminology (such as "baton zone," "baton touch," "400 meter relay," etc.), equipment, facilities, judges, etc. These all form the unique society of the relay.

Shotput-ness (the shotput human)

Among the types of the track and field human, there is the shotput human. The shotput human forms the unique society of the shotput. In the society of the shotput, there are equipment (the shotput, the circle, etc.), facilities, judges, and rules. These are necessary factors in the society of the shotput which cannot be omitted. It is within the society of these factors that the shotput human acts and exists.

In this way, in every country in the world, the track and field human exists in the aspects of every country in the world. Also, while responding to the changes that occur in the passing of time, it forms the unique society of track and field. Thus, the track and field human exists together with the cultural aspects of track and field competition.

If in the future, there appear track and field events like the running high jump or the discus throw (which involve the one-sided actions of trying to separate from the ground) which can be performed by a group, then we can add them to this chart. The actions of a group in the running high jump, for instance, might be an example of this.

To summarize up to this point, I have shown proof for my hypothesis of the phenomenon of track and field competition, which will confirm the scholarship of track and field studies and demonstrate the essence of the phenomenon of track and field competition. The hypothesis to which I refer, once again, says that when a human performs track and field competition, the human does not become a

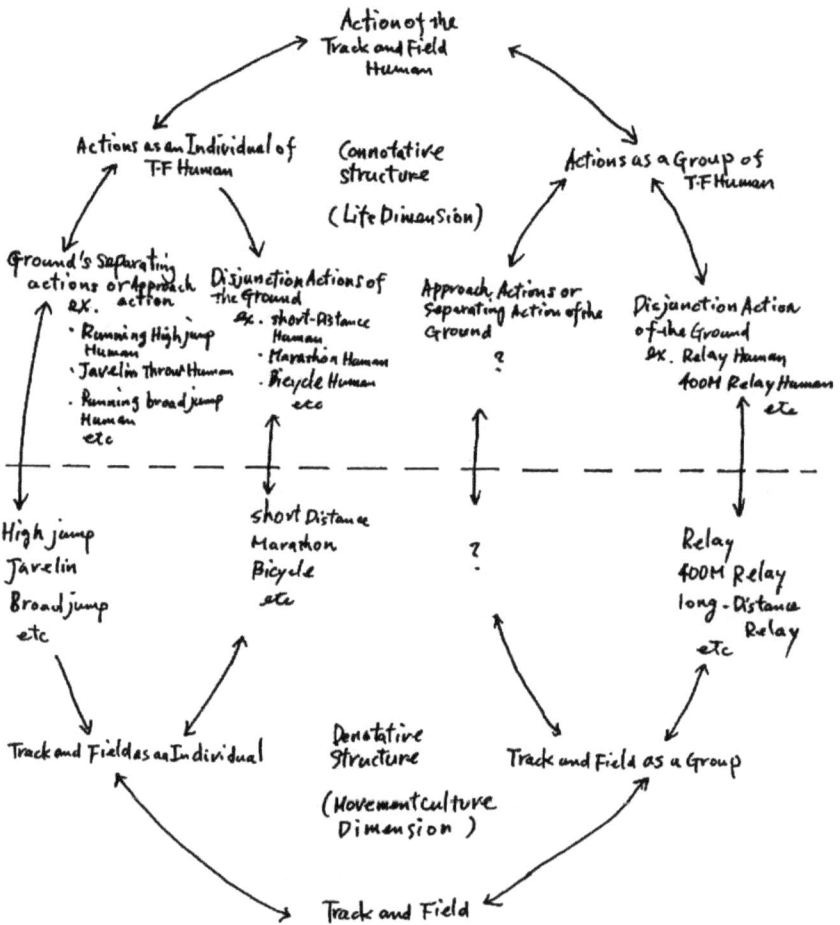

Figure 16. The Cultural Existence of the Track and Field Human

human-the human becomes a track and field human. I have explained this proof through the aspects of the phenomenon of track and field competition, using the phrase "track and field human," in this ontology. More specifically, as a result, we can say (as is stated by the hypothesis that I have presented) that track and field competition is itself conduct for the becoming of a track and field human.

Now, through the proof of this hypothesis, it has become possible for us to establish track and field studies in every country in the world. Therefore, I will continue by presenting the teleology and the methodology of the track and field human. If we are to proceed to establish track and field studies, then it is imperative that we develop the theory in the teleology of the track and field human.

6

The Teleology of the Track and Field Human

What is the purpose of the track and field human? It is necessary to begin by asking this question. It is clear that the track and field human exists in every country in the world, and, furthermore, within physical education classes. I think that it is natural and logical that the teleology should be derived from the realistic existence of the track and field human. Therefore, it is not an overstatement to say that everything I have presented up to this point has served to form the foundation that will form the purpose of the track and field human. Thus, I will now be able to go on to write about the purpose of all types of the track and field human in every country in the world-all types of the track and field human image-from the existence of all types of the track and field human in every country in the world. The track and field human image is the ideal of existence, and because this is actually rooted in purpose, each type of the track and field human image appears differently in each country in the world, in different sexes, in different races, in different regions, in different environments, etc. Also, I would like to point out once again that the track and field human image is within the phenomenon of track and field that occurs in every country in the world, and that this is not delimited to either practice or theory. It can be applied to the regions in every country in the world in which track and field events are dealt with in scholastic physical education. Also, the track and field human image, which I will go on to present, changes realistically with the passing of each era. It will be necessary for the physical education and sports studies researchers concerned with all types of track and field competition in every country in the world (such as physical education and sports philosophy, physical education and sports psychology, physical education and sports physiology, physical education and sports sociology, physical education and sports history, etc.) to achieve the realization of all types of the track and field human image in the phenomenon of track and field competition and in the practice that occurs in track and field events.

The track and field human image is the purpose in track and field competition and in the practice of all types of track and field events, but it is necessary to demonstrate to what in reality this refers. Specifically, this refers to the ideal existence in track and field practice where the actions of the track and field human as a movement human and the actions of the track and field human as the supportive movement of the ground mutually act together to produce superior actions.

In the nature of the substance of the track and field human image, there are two different qualities. These two qualities dynamically act together to form a solid track and field human image. First, there is the universal quality of the teleology, which is common to any era, to any place, and to any country. For example, the superior actions of the movement human and the ground in track and field competition, namely the striving for the realization of the realization of the track and field human image, are common to any place and any country, even though differences may exists in ideas, race, culture, and history. This is the universal quality.

The other quality is the variable, concrete purpose of the track and field human, which differs in different countries, different eras, different societies, different ages, different sexes, and other differences. In each country there is uniqueness in the country's history, ideas, culture, etc. The track and field human image of a certain era in each country reflects the aspects of that era. In addition, from the standpoint of age, there are differences between all types of the track and field human image for children and all types of the track and field human image for old people. Likewise, from the standpoint of sex, there are differences between all types of the track and field human image for males and all types of the track and field human image for females. There are many ways that these track and field human images differ. They are certainly not all alike. As opposed to the universal content of the purpose of the track and field human previously presented, this points to the variable, concrete content of the purpose of the track and field human. The construction of the teleology of the track and field human rests on the dynamic, mutually supportive relationship between these two in which both support and are supported. The former track and field human image is the purpose of the track and field human, while the latter is the goal of the track and field human. The difference between these two words demonstrates the difference between the universal purpose and the variable purpose. While the content of the purpose serves as the nucleus of the track and field human image, the content of the goal envelops it. In the dynamic relationship between these two, it assumes an abstract/concrete, concrete/abstract character. Therefore, this teleology provides a unified quality in which the track and field human image transcends the realities of time, nationality, age, sex, etc., while at the same time it is able to view these realities as realities. The chart below will summarize this idea (see Figure 17).

Of what type of content is the purpose of the track and field human, namely the track and field human image composed? Next I will go on to explain this point.

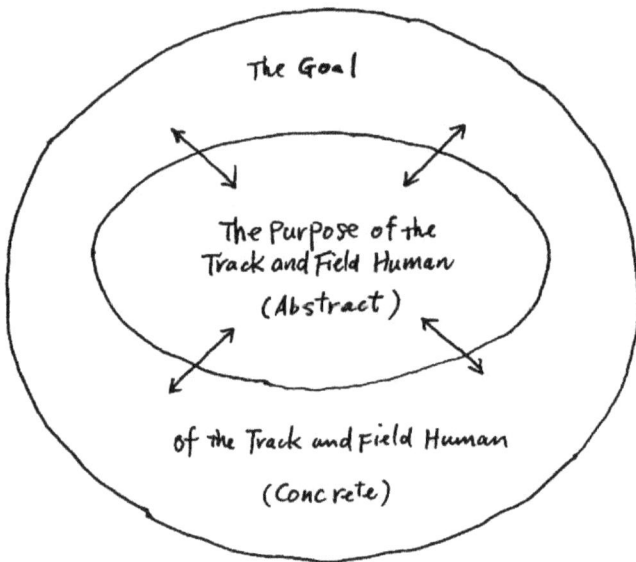

Figure 17.

The structure of the track and field human image presents two types of structures: a connotative structure and a denotative structure which together form a dynamic union. There are actions of the various different element images that as a whole act ideally. If we broadly divide these ideal elements, they come into being from the connotative structure or the denotative structure (see Figure 18).

THE CONNOTATIVE STRUCTURE

In the actions acting in the track and field human image, f there is an image of connotative structure. This acts in a manner that is the origin of the generation of the image of denotative structure, and therefore these actions are vitally important. The image of connotative structure itself is formed from the various element images that become the many different ideals. It arises from the life energy image, which is an ideal from physical education and sports nutrition studies and physical education and sports hygiene studies, the body image, the mind image (the mind-body image), etc., which are ideals from physical education and sports philosophy, the body strength image, the flexibility image, the physique image, the physical condition image (the health image), etc., which are ideals from physical education and sports physiology, the morale image, the flexibility image, the character image, the condition of character image (the health image), etc., which are ideals from physical education and sports psychology, etc. When the physical education and sports studies researchers in every country in the world elucidate the realistic existence of the track and field human, as a result of the their actual proof, these images of the connotative structure of the track and field human will be concretely living and acting ideals. Every physical education and sports studies researcher in every country in the world must advance this research of purpose in order to I flesh out the content of these words regarding the various elements and to further the perception of these as words of a living reality. Why are the educational ministries of every country in the world conducting and practicing all types of track and field in scholastic physical education? As a result of the research from the various fields of physical education and sports studies, namely physical education and sports philosophy, physical education and sports psychology, physical education and sports physiology, physical education and sports sociology, physical

Figure 18. Track and Field Human Image.

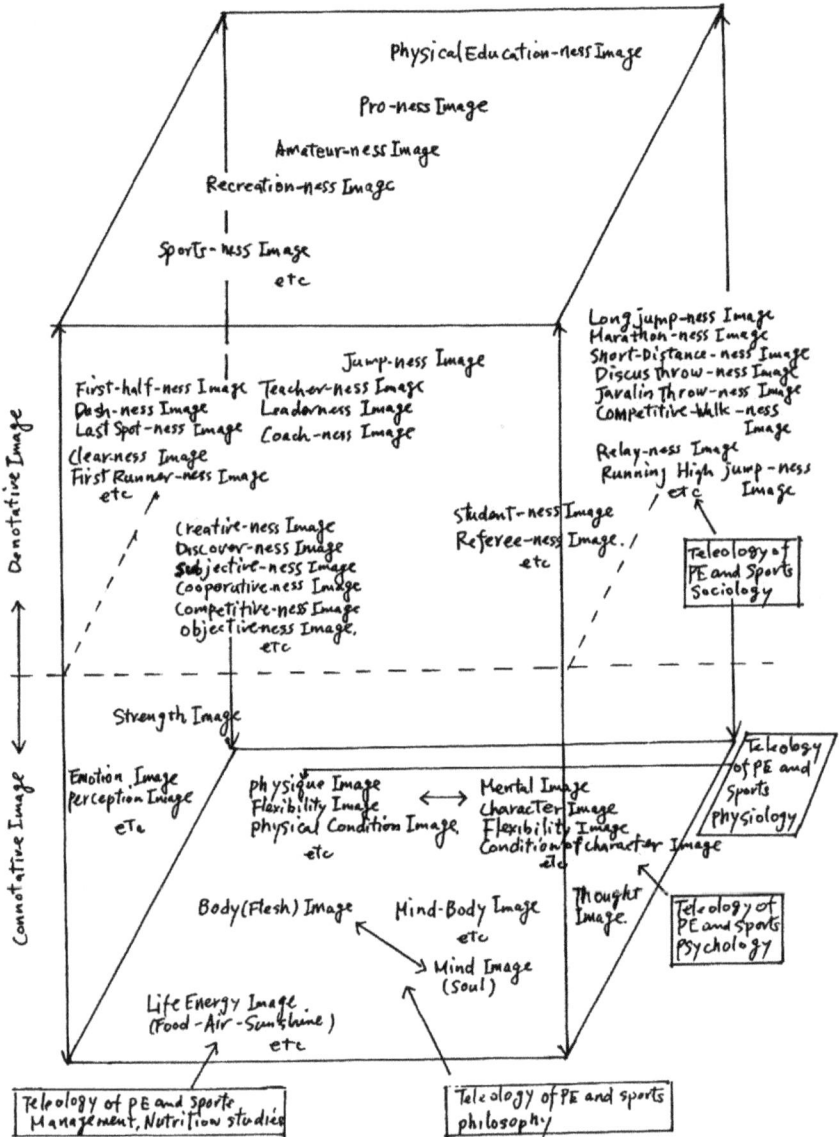

Physical Education-ness Image

Pro-ness Image

Amateur-ness Image

Recreation-ness Image

Sports-ness Image
etc

Long jump-ness Image
Marathon-ness Image
Short-Distance-ness Image
Discus throw-ness Image
Javalin throw-ness Image
Competitive walk-ness Image

Relay-ness Image
Running High Jump-ness Image
etc

Jump-ness Image

First-half-ness Image   Teacher-ness Image
Dash-ness Image   Leader-ness Image
Last Spot-ness Image   Coach-ness Image
Clear-ness Image
First Runner-ness Image
etc

Creative-ness Image
Discover-ness Image
Subjective-ness Image
Cooporative-ness Image
Competitive-ness Image
objectiveness Image,
etc

Student-ness Image
Referee-ness Image.
etc

Teleology of
PE and Sports
Sociology

Denotative Image

Strength Image

Emotion Image
Perception Image
etc

physique Image
Flexibility Image
physical Condition Image
etc

Mental Image
Character Image
Flexibility Image
Condition of character Image
etc

Teleology
of PE and
Sports
physiology

Connotative Image

Body (Flesh) Image   Mind-Body Image
etc

Mind Image
(Soul)

Thought
Image.

Teleology of
PE and Sports
Psychology

Life Energy Image.
(Food - Air - Sunshine)
etc

Teleology of PE and Sports
Management, Nutrition studies

Teleology of PE and sports
philosophy

* In physical education and sports, the track and field human forms the special society of track and field competition and acts ideally in a unique way. At the same time, it is restricted in a unique way to exist ideally.

96

education and sports history, etc., this question can be answered directly. For example, from physical education and sports philosophy, we can say that all types of track and field competition are being practiced in scholastic physical education in order to realize the body image and the mind image of all types of track and field human. It is up to the research of the physical education and sports philosophers to explain the content of the body image and the mind image.

The content of all of the various partial element images that were presented here will be ideal content that is established by the actual proof of the specialized researchers in physical education and sports studies. Meanwhile, among the elements in the image of connotative structure, they will be performing superior actions.

Also, these are the various elements that do superior actions in the image of the denotative structure as well. For example, the image of body strength is the superior inner actions of body strength itself, acting in superior actions in relation to the various elements, such as morale, flexibility, cooperativeness, competitiveness, physical condition, creativeness, etc.

As is shown previously, the image of the connotative structure in the track and field human image is the entirety of the various element images of the connotative structure that have been amassed by the physical education and sports studies researchers in every country in the world and the physical education and sports studies research of every era. However, this image of connotative structure acts not only as the image of connotative structure, but is also an image of connotative structure that acts on the image of denotative structure. SO, what kind of substance is in the ideal images that make up the image of the denotative structure of the track and field human image? I will now go on to deal with this question.

THE IMAGE OF DENOTATIVE STRUCTURE

In the actions of the track and field human image as a track and field human image, there is an image of denotative structure. In the ideal image that is generated from the image of connotative structure, the origin of the establishment of the image of the denotative structure is included. Inside the denotative structure itself, which acts as the denotative structure, are the actions of the various element images.

Looking from the specialized point of view of the physical education and sports sociologists and scholastic physical education, and considering the existential direction of the track and field human, if an inquiry is made to determine the ideal images of that existence, then in the following way, the idealistic elements of the denotative structure become visible. The image of sports-ness, the image of physical education-ness, the image of amateur-ness, the image of professional-ness, the image of trim-ness, the image of recreation-ness, the image of teacher-ness, the image of student-ness, the image of leader- -ness, the image of follower-ness, the image of coach-ness, the image of short distance-ness, the image of running high jump-ness, the image of marathon-ness, the image of shotput-ness, the image of javelin throw-ness, the image of pole vault-ness, the image of creativeness, the image of cooperativeness, the image of competitive-ness, the image of discovery-ness, the image of dash-ness, the image of last spot-ness, the image of broad jump-ness, the image of the fourth runner-ness, the image of judge-ness, the image of bicycle-ness, the image of objectiveness, the image of subjectiveness, etc. From the above kinds of images of elements, the image of the denotative structure in the track and field human image is formed. The various images of elements above are the various aspects of the track and field human image, and they are things that have been culled from researchers in physical education and sports sociology and scholastic physical education. Then, the images of the various elements in the denotative structure act in a way that promotes the idealistic condition of the connotative structure, while at the same time they are the superior denotative elements that act in a way that promotes the idealistic condition of the elements in the image of the denotative structure. Therefore, each of the elements in the denotative structure themselves are living elements that are superior and act ideally.

In the preceding manner, the track and field human image itself is the actual purpose of the existence of the track and field human in every country in the world. Therefore, this is regulated by the existence of the track and field human, and in reality there is a purpose in straining to derive the track and field human image from this existence. For example, in order to explain this track and field human image as a track and field human image in reality, we can divide the track and field human image into its various different types, such as the marathon human image, the 100 meter human image, the hurdler human image, the running high jump human image, the shotput human image, the javelin throw human image, the bicycle human image, and so on. We can concretely express the goal of the track and field human if we look, for instance, at the running high jump human from various points of view. From the point of view of school level, there are the elementary school running high jump human image and the high school running high jump human image. From the point of view of sex, there are the male running high jump human image and the female running high jump human image. From the point of view of nationality, there are the running high jump human image as an American, the running high jump human image as a Soviet, and so on. In other words, because the existence of all types of the track and field human in every country of the world is different, the purpose of the track and field human can be materialized as different goals. Thus, as the existence of all types of the track and field human is different in every country in the world, the purpose of the track and field human is materialized as a different objective. On the other hand, while the track and field human image can make as its purpose the various unique track and field human images of each country in the world, from a global, humanistic, common point of view, it can also present a purpose that is the track and field human image as a world citizen. Provided that the existence of all types of the track and field human practicing all kinds of track and field events in all places around the world can be con- firmed, this purpose can be erected as a common purpose of all types of the track and field human as a world citizen.

Above I have presented the purpose of the track and field human, or more specifically, the substance of the track and field human image. As a result, we have reached a point at which the following kinds of questions can be answered:

Question 1: Why are the educational ministries of every country in the world practicing all types of track and field events in scholastic physical education?
Answer: All types of track and field are being practiced in scholastic

physical education in every country in the world in order to realize all types of the track and field human image as the peoples of every country in the world.

Question 2: Why are the educational ministries of every country in the world doing classes on the theory concerning all types of track and field competition in scholastic education?
Answer: This is so that in the scholastic education of every country in the world, physical education teachers will show the peaceful practice of all types of track and field competition to students, and so that they will explain the practice of all types of track and field competition to the students and the students will understand them.

Question 3: Why is the IOC doing all types of track and field competition in the Olympics?
Answer: The IOC is practicing all types of track and field competition so that, in the Olympics, all types of the track and field human image will be realized. Also, this practice will translate into world peace.

Question 4: Why are the physical education and sports researchers of every country in the world conducting research in fields such as physical education and sports psychology, physical education and sports philosophy, physical education and sports physiology, physical education and sports history, physical education and sports sociology, etc.?
Answer: This is so that in the place of the track and field practice in every country in the world, the track and field human image of every country in the world will be realized. It is also necessary in order to construct the theory.

Question 5: Why must a World Physical Education and Sports Academy be established?
Answer: Relying on the development of this type of research, the track and field human image in every country in the world and the track and field human image of each age of mankind will be constructed, thus developing the guarantee of peace in every country

and world peace. Also, the academy will nurture physical education and sports researchers who will contribute to peace in every country and to world peace.

Question 6: Why must a Physical Education and Sports Academy be established in every country in the world?

Answer: Physical education and sports researchers (from every field) are necessary to construct the ball game theory in every country and in order to guarantee that the practice of ball games in every country in the world is a peaceful practice. They will promote research with meaning that contributes to peace in their countries. At the same time, it is also necessary to nurture national doctorates in every country, and to nurture physical education and sports researchers that will contribute to world peace through the ball game studies research in every country.

In addition, any questions concerning the purpose of formation related to all types of ball games in every country in the world can be answered from the Teleology of the Track and Field Human. Also, through the purpose, it is necessary to go on to develop support for peace in every country and world peace.

Furthermore, from the presentations of the Ontology and Teleology of the Track and Field Human in every country in the world, we must now go on to develop the Methodology of the Track and Field human in every country in the world by which the existence of the track and field human in every country in the world realizes the track and field human image of every country in the world. This will deal with the method by which the existence of the track and field human in every country in the world realizes the track and field human image. The methodology will be organically connected to the ontology and the teleology, and will have the unique quality that it will work together with them. This kind of undertaking will serve to realize the establishment of universal track and field theory, which will unite all countries in the world.

7

The Methodology of the Track and Field Human

The methodology of the track and field human is an original theoretical area that deals with the actions of both the movement human (the track and field human) and the ground sides of the track and field human in the phenomenon of all types of track and field competition. These two sides (the movement human and the ground), which are referred to directly by the term "track and field human," can be said to be able, depending on how they dynamically work together to emphasize an intent on harmony, to realize the track and field human image. For example, if we emphasize the ground, only the ability required for the ground is required of the movement human. On the other hand, if we emphasize the movement human, only the ability required for the movement human is required of the ground. Therefore, achieving the required ability that is possible when both sides accept each other's demands is imperative. This type of method is the only advanced method by which the track and field human image can be realized. Toward that end, there are notably two methodologies: one in relation to time, and one in relation to space. The former considers the experience of becoming a track and field human in terms of time, while the latter considers the experience of becoming a track and field human in terms of space. Therefore, the method that realizes the track and field human image must give the appropriate weight to experience in time and experience in space in becoming a track and field human.

THE THEORETICAL FOUNDATION AND GROUNDS FOR THE FORMATION OF THE TRACK AND FIELD HUMAN METHODOLOGY

Before presenting the Methodology of the Track and Field Human, it is necessary to first make clear the reasons why it is possible to present such a methodology. In order to do this, we must look at the theoretical foundation and the grounds for the methodology. The theoretical foundation for the formation of the Methodology of the Track and Field Human relies on the Educational, Social, and Movement-Cultural Ontologies of the Track and Field Human and the Teleology of the Track and Field Human already presented. The grounds for the formation of this methodology are the fact that, in scholastic physical education in every country around the world, track and field competition is being practiced. The former is based on the development of the theory, while the latter comes from the practice of track and field competition.

THE CHARACTER OF THE METHODOLOGY OF THE TRACK AND FIELD HUMAN

There are two characters associated with the content of the Methodology of the Track and Field Human. First, it is an unchangeable, universal, abstract methodology, applicable to any country at any time. Second, as countries and times change, it is a concrete, realistic methodology that changes accordingly. The Methodology of the Track and Field Human is constructed with the former at the core, while the latter surrounds it, both working together to preserve the relationship. More specifically, the former is the area of the methodology based on the common qualities of all countries and constructed by the physical education and sports researchers of every country in the world so that the practice of track and field competition in scholastic physical education in every country in the world serves to realize the track and field human image. Meanwhile, the latter is the area of the methodology that has the quality that it grasps the differences in the realistic aspects of the track and field human, i.e., country, time, age, sex, school, etc., as differences in realistic aspects.

ELEMENTS OF THE FORMATION OF THE CONTENTS OF THE METHODOLOGY OF THE TRACK AND FIELD HUMAN

In regard to the formation of the Methodology of the Track and

Field Human, both the theoretical foundation and the practical grounds have already been presented. However, I believe that the latter, the practical grounds, gives an extraordinarily important reason for the formation of the Methodology of the Track and Field Human. Namely, because of the existence of the practice of track and field competition in physical education programs, the existence of the practice of track and field competition in society, and because of the existence of physical education teachers, mentors, pupils, and students who play a function in society, the need for the Methodology of the Track and Field Human becomes apparent.

In that case, physical education teachers and mentors are those who lead students to become track and field humans and realize the track and field human image, while students and followers who receive all forms of track and field education are those who look toward becoming all forms of track and field humans and realizing all forms of the track and field human image. Therefore, the human relationships of the teachers and mentors and students and followers in the phenomenon of the track and field competition will all become the track and field human and realize the track and field human image. These are mutual relationships that exist to realize the track and field human image.

Those fostering the track and field human have experience in the past of fully becoming a track and field human in order to realize the track and field human image. They are those who possess the leadership qualifications to be able to realize the track and field human image. On the other hand, those becoming track and field humans must receive leadership in order to realize the track and field human image. They are those of whom study ability is demanded.

With the relationship between physical education teachers, who try to realize the track and field human image and foster track and field humans, and students, who study while looking toward becoming track and field humans and realizing the track and field human image, as the grounds, the various structural elements of the methodology of the various kinds of track and field humans are formed. Specifically, these elements include study, leadership, evaluation, curriculum, educational resources, study ability, study processes, leadership ability, skill, etc., Classifying these elements into large groups, we may divide them into study, leadership, and educational resources. The terms "skill," "study ability," "study processes," etc. are all terms connected with the student or follower becoming a track and field human and trying to realize the track and field human image, and are therefore "study" terms. The terms "leadership ability," "evaluation," "curriculum," etc., are all terms connected with the teachers and mentors trying to realize the track and field human image and turn their students into track and field humans, and are therefore "leadership" terms. Finally, that which brings the leadership and study together at the place of the track and field competition is the educational resources. The structural elements of the Methodology of the Track and Field Human are systematized in the manner described in figure 19.

Figure 19. The Structural Elements of the Methodology of the Track and Field Human

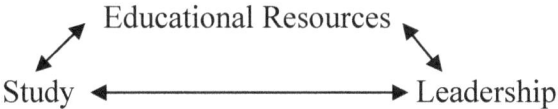

Study. This is the state of those becoming track and field humans in which they learn all of the various things they must learn from those helping them to become track and field humans in order to realize the track and field human image. Also, we will call "students" those who, under the supervision of those fostering the track and field human, strive to learn that which they need to become a track and field human.

Furthermore, "study ability" is ability that students possess to learn all the constructive knowledge required in order to become a track and field human and realize the track and field human image. "Skill" is a part of study ability, and is the condition of the mastery of the necessary techniques required to become a track and field human and realize the track and field human image. Also, "study process" is the process by which, under the leadership of those fostering the track and field human, those becoming track and field humans learn all of the relevant knowledge.

Leadership. This is defined as the leading of those who will become track and field humans by those who will foster their becoming track and field humans by giving them all the various knowledge they will need toward the goal of realizing the track and field human image. "Leadership ability" is the ability of those fostering track and field humans, with the goal of realizing the track and field human image, develop to fully those becoming track and field humans. The "leadership process" is the process by which those fostering track and field humans, with the goal of realizing the track and field human image, lead those becoming track and field humans. Furthermore, "evaluation" is the process by which those fostering track and field humans decide what level those becoming track and field humans have reached and how far they have advanced in approaching the realization of the track and field human image. "Curriculum" is the study route through which those fostering track and field humans lead those becoming track and field humans in order to realize the track and field human image.

Educational Resources. A collective use of this term refers to all materials that fostering track and field humans use to lead future track and field humans to realize the track and field human image, along with all study materials used by those becoming track and field humans whose aim is to realize the track and field human image. Therefore, the educational resources play the role of intermediary in the formation of the leadership and study of the track and field human, and are a necessary methodological element in the realization of the track and field human image. The educational resources include natural educational resources and man-made educational resources. The former are sunshine, air, weather (clear, rain, snow, clouds), air pressure (wind), water (water in a pool), earth (ground), etc. The latter include hurdles, baton, line, lighting, bar, stand, soft mat, goal post, pistol, blocks, circle, javelin, shotput, discus, hammer, indoor track, etc. Therefore, in the broad sense of the word, "educational resources" refer to the combination of natural educational resources and man-made natural resources, but when taken in the narrow sense of the word, refers mostly to man-made educational resources.

THE CONSTRUCTION METHOD OF THE
METHODOLOGY OF THE TRACK AND FIELD HUMAN

It is imperative that we use the terminology of the structural elements of the Methodology of the Track and Field Human, namely study (skill, study process, etc.), leadership (evaluation, curriculum, leadership process, leadership ability, etc.) and educational resources in order to realize the track and field human image. However, it is also necessary to answer the question of how the content of these elements can be given substance. I will now present these kinds of problems related to the construction of the Methodology of the Track and Field Human.

From the standpoint of those dealing with fundamental theory of physical education studies, it is possible to construct a methodology that answers these kinds of questions. The Methodology of the Track and Field Human should use the original specialized vocabulary from each specialized area of physical education, and considering study, leadership, and educational resources, etc. we can create a separate methodology from each field of physical education that serves to realize every partial image of the track and field human that is derived from that field. In regard to the Methodology of the Track and Field Human from physical education physiology, for instance, while considering study, leadership, and educational resources, we can construct an original methodology, using the specialized terms of physiology, such as strength, physique, health, and flexibility, that serves to realize the strength image, the physique image, the health image, and the flexibility image of the track and field human.

Likewise, in regard to the Methodology of the Track and Field Human from physical education psychology, while considering study, leadership, and educational resources, we can construct an original methodology, using the specialized terms of psychology, such as character, morale, health, flexibility, etc., that serves to realize the character image, the morale image, the health image, and the flexibility image of the track and field human. In regard to the Methodology of the Track and Field Human from physical education philosophy, while considering study, leadership, and educational resources, we can construct an original methodology, using the specialized terms of philosophy, such as mind, body, the mind-body relationship, soul, flesh, etc., that serves to realize the mind image, the body image, the mind-body image, the soul image, and the flesh image of the track and field human. In regard to the Methodology of the Track and Field Human from physical education educational science, while considering study, leadership, and educational resources, we can construct an original methodology, using the specialized terms of educational science, such as creativity, subjectivity, objectivity, cooperation, competition, etc. that serves to realize the creativity image, the subjectivity image, the objectivity image, the cooperation image, and the competition image of the track and field human. In regard to the Methodology of the Track and Field Human from physical education sociology, while considering study, leadership, and educational resources, we can construct an original methodology, using the specialized terms of sociology, such as dash, last spot, 100 meter run, running high jump, pole vault, javelin throw, marathon, middle-distance, hammer throw, etc., that serves to realize the dash image, last spot image, 100meter run image, running high jump image, pole vault image, javelin throw image, marathon image, middle-distance image, hammer throw image, etc., of the track and field human. In regard to the Methodology of the Track and Field Human from biomechanics, while considering study, leadership, and educational resources, we can construct an original methodology, using the specialized terms of biomechanics that serves to realize the grasping image, the throwing image, the jumping image, the running image, the pushing image, the kicking image, etc., of the track and field human.

Moreover, the construction of the original methodologies of the track and field human for each of these specialized fields of physical education must be living, changing entities, taking into account the realistic existence of things such as nationality, race, age, sex, etc., to always be the best methodology for physical education researchers of the present time. Therefore, research specialists in each field of physical education must, while referring to the knowledge in physical education history for advice, construct separate methodologies responsible for each specialized field.

In the above manner, it is possible to construct a Methodology of the Track and Field Human for every country in the world.

8

The Path Toward an Olympics in Which the Physical Education and Sports studies Researchers of Each Country in the World Compete

CONCLUSION

Up to this point, I have developed this theory from the ontology to the teleology, and finally to the methodology. With this, we have reached the stage of the completion of Track and Field Theory (World United). Using Track and Field Theory, which is simply a collective term for the theories concerning every type of track and field competition, we can go on to promote the formation of scholarship in areas such as marathon studies, short-distance studies, running high jump studies, javelin throw studies, pole vault studies, etc. This will be formed as a theory of track and field studies dealing with the practice of each type of track and field competition.

This track and field theory will appear as the fundamental theory for the purpose of constructing track and field studies in every country in the world. Without regard to the differences of history, thought, culture, etc. that exist between countries, this will be a theory that will be applicable to every country in which all types of track and field competition are practiced in physical education and in society. This Track and Field Theory will deal with the whole theories of track and field competition studies, while also dealing with the partial theories from every field of physical education and sports studies, namely physical education and sports philosophy, physical education and sports psychology, physical education and sports physiology, physical education and sports sociology, biomechanics, etc. While consulting the facts in physical education and sports history and using the specialized terminology of every field, it will elucidate the realistic phenomenon of each type of track and field competition. It will be able to confirm the scholarship as necessary to unify, from each specialized field, the ontologies, teleologies, and methodologies of all types of track and field humans in every country in the world, in every era. At the same time, these partial theories will fit into the entire theory, namely Track and Field Theory, and promote the establishment of scholarship in marathon studies, short-distance studies, running high jump studies, discus throw studies, hurdle studies, etc. With the completion of this theory, the question Why are all types of track and field competition being conducted by the educational ministries in scholastic physical education in every country in the world?" will be answered from the partial theories that are put forth from the research in each of the specialized fields of physical education and sports studies. Therefore, the various specialized research in physical education and sports studies based on the Track and Field Theory will be important social and nationalistic research. Thus, to those who achieve success with partial theories, it will be possible to award a physical education and sports studies doctorate (national doctorate) degree. Furthermore, the grounds and theoretical basis for the worthiness of these partial theories of the doctorate degree can be explained to general society and guaranteed through Track and Field Theory. In other words, the doctorate degree in physical education and sports studies will gain social and international trust when evaluated as being objectively responsible, both within the country and without.

This Track and Field Theory refers to the criteria and principles necessary for healthy physical education and sports research in every country. Thus, it deals with important and detailed rules to insure the healthy state of physical education and sports research in the country of each physical education and sports researcher. If the countries of the world, or even some country, tries to conduct research concerning track and field competition without paying attention to this Track and Field Theory, several severe problems will result, including tasteless and dry research that is void of knowledge and isolated from the phenomenon of track and field competition, a lack of connection between the physical education and sports researcher and his nation and society, and chaos stemming from confusion of knowledge. Thus, physical education and sports research will surely fall into the trap of conducting physical education and sports research for the sake of spending (wasting) money. Therefore, we must fairly evaluate whether or not countries are applying this Track and Field Theory and whether or not they are conducting true physical education and sports research. Above all, in order to conduct physical education and sports research, we must recognize physical education and sports theory as necessary, and from its principles develop research. Without physical education and sports theory, there can be no physical education and sports research.

In presenting this Track and Field Theory to the physical education and sports researchers of every country in the world, I hope to insure a common object of research for the physical education and sports researchers in each country. I would like to make sure that each researcher is self-conscious in advancing research. In addition, I hope to demonstrate the social responsibility of physical education and sports researchers. In performing this role, I am contributing to society and to physical education. Also, this effort will lead us to the path to world peace and peace in every country, and with this presentation the first step has been taken toward this development. When the physical education and sports researchers in every country in the world awaken national consciousness and world consciousness, social unity, national unity, and even world unity will be born. Eventually, this theory, as a theory of the Olympics which deals with the practice of the Olympics, will lead to progress in the direction of the establishment of a World Physical Education and Sports Academy (ICHPERSD in USA). At the same time, we must promise that physical education and sports studies will not be governed by other areas of scholarship, but will crystallize as an independent study on its own.

The path toward world physical education and sports studies is long and steep, but if the physical education and sports researchers of every country in the world arise as self-conscious physical education and sports scholars, we shall start out on this natural path–the path toward the establishment of a World Physical Education and Sports Academy (ICHPERSD in USA). Eventually, it is possible that there may be a World Physical Education and Sports Scholars' Olympics, but, for now, this is one theory in physical education and sports theory.

Part III

Theory of International Swimming Studies for the Achievement of Peace

1

A Word from the Author

This theory puts forth physical education and sports research as research for the purpose of supporting world peace and peace within every country in the world. This fundamental theory will establish the World Physical and Sports Academy (ICHPERSD in USA), which will go on to forge the policies of physical education and sports academies in every country in the world.

2

Establishing the Hypothesis for Creating Swimming Studies

The following questions were the motivations for the attempt to create this Theory of International Swimming Studies for the Achievement of Peace:

1. Why, in the scholastic physical education programs of the education ministries of each country in the world, are teachers using all types of swimming as the educational resource to lead students?
2. Why are all types of swimming being brought together and performed at the Olympics founded by Baron Pierre de Coubertin of France?
3. Why are the physical education and sports researchers of each country in the world conducting research concerning all types of swimming?
4. Why are physical education teachers and physical education and sports researchers of every country in the world conducting classes in every school concerning the theory of all types of swimming?
5. Why should research concerning swimming be considered physical education studies or sports studies research?
6. Why is research concerning swimming worthy of a physical education and sports studies doctorate degree?

Presently, there exists no theory from the world's physical education and sports studies research that can answer these fundamental problems of swimming research. For those of us who pursue such a fundamental theory of physical education and sports studies research, this is an urgent problem for which we must find a solution. These questions must become the motivation for our research-the point of embarkation at which we begin our inquiries. They will be the energy source for our continued research.

In creating this "Theory of International Swimming Studies for the Achievement of Peace," one term will be used throughout as a building block. It will refer to the joint subject formed by the human (self) and some other (either another person or some other thing); a subject that acts together both passively and actively. This is the *swimming human* (which refers to the joint subject composed of water and human). The term *swimming human* includes all types of concrete swimming humans, such as the butterfly human, the crawl human, the diving human, the backstroke human, the breaststroke human, the synchronized swimming human, canoe human, boat human, etc. We will use the term *swimming human* to refer to all of these collectively. This term refers directly to the dynamic existence itself of the human and the water that are found in the swimming phenomenon.

The term *swimming human* is used quite a bit from here on, but to what in reality does this term refer? It is necessary to explain this clearly and in detail. The object to which the term *swimming human* refers is the water (in the phenomenon of swimming, the object of the actions of the movement human) and the movement human (in the phenomenon of swimming, the object of the actions of the water) in the phenomenon of swimming or phenomena in which water is dealt with. Thus, the movement human is a movement human in relation to water, and the water is water in relation to the movement human. Together, they share necessary and indispensable common ground. This common ground is in the acting together as a joint subject of water and human, and in the forming of the dynamic phenomenon of swimming. However, if we look objectively, we see that the actions of the swimming human as the actions of the water and the actions of the swimming human as a movement human are completely different, and we can make a distinction between them. Therefore, from here on in the development of this theory I will simply use the expression swimming human to refer directly to both the movement human part of the swimming human and the water actions part of the swimming human. Only in cases in which there must explicitly be a distinction between the swimming human as a movement human and the swimming human as the actions of water will use these expressions.

Therefore, I would like the reader to understand the fact that the expression *swimming human* refers to both the movement human and water actions sides of the swimming human. If we do not use this method of expression, the expressions will not be applicable to the factual phenomenon of swimming and we will be left with a theory that is removed from actual practice. Also, it serves to make a distinction between the existence experienced in the special world of swimming (which must be dealt with by physical education and sports studies) and other existences, and to express the special uniqueness in that world. Meanwhile, it serves to facilitate the construction of a theory concerning the special world of swimming.

Thus, I have designed the following hypothesis concerning the phenomenon of swimming (which occurs in every country in the world): *When a human practices swimming, the human does not become a human, the human becomes a* **swimming human**, *acting in a way that forms the special society of swimming. This is because "doing" is "doing"–"doing" is not "not doing."*

There is now a problem that lies before us. In what ways do the phenomena of swimming and the phenomena in which water is dealt with (which occur in many aspects in every country in the world) appear as lively phenomena before our eyes? It is imperative that we find clear answers to this question.

Thus, in order to answer this question, I have attempted to elucidate the living phenomenon of swimming, based on an analysis of insight and an integrated judgment method. Using this approach, I believe that the existential essence of the phenomenon of swimming and the phenomena in which water is dealt with appear in the aspects of the swimming human. Furthermore, the nonessential part of the existence appears in the various aspects of the dance human, the ball human, the track and field human, etc. I believe that all of these together form the living phenomenon of the swimming human which appears before our eyes. Figure 20 gives a graphic explanation of this concept.

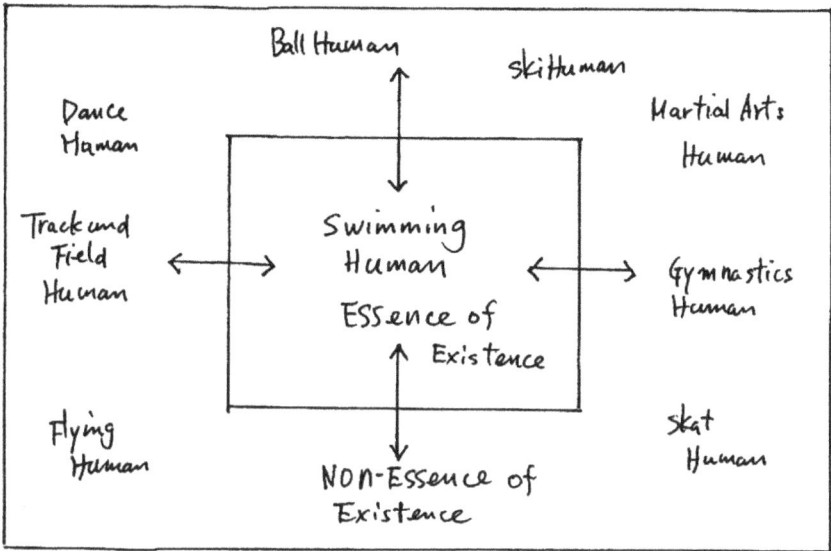

Figure 20.

Therefore, these can be seen as the vital structural factors that form the living phenomenon of swimming. The most important of these are the dynamic actions that exist in the relation of the human and the water. These are the existential essence of the aspects of the swimming human. Meanwhile, there are actions that exist on the perimeter that also act to form the swimming human, such as the aspects of the dance human, aspects of the ball human, aspects of the gymnastics human, etc. The living phenomenon of the swimming human is supported by all of these actions that help to form it. For example, in the phenomenon of swimming, there are separate actions that act as the existence of the self. These actions can be described as the nonessence of the swimming human, and they include the relation between the swimming human and another surface, the relation to an image, the relation to a ball, etc. They also include the relation to equipment, as in the case of the gymnastics human (for example, the actions of the diving human when acting in relation to the diving board). Therefore, the existential essence of the phenomenon of swimming is composed of the actions that stem from the existence of the swimming human. Furthermore, along with these actions that stem from the existence of the swimming human, there are actions that stem from a different kind of existence, namely those of the dance human, the ball human, the gymnastics human, the track and field human, etc. All of these mix together to form the phenomenon of swimming as a living entity.

Thus, the entirety of the phenomenon of swimming that appears before our eyes is the swimming human, the living actions of the human and the water in the phenomenon. This truly exists, and acts as an essential existence forming all types of the swimming phenomenon. In other words, it is the "producer" that puts forth the phenomenon of swimming and creates its special properties. However, the swimming human in the phenomenon of swimming is not simply used for the human and the water in the phenomenon of swimming. In the case of synchronized swimming, there are relationships between the human and an image. Furthermore, in the case of the diving human, there are relationships with equipment like those of the gymnastics human, and glimpses of the track and field human can be seen as the diver gets his running start.

All types of swimming (and living phenomena in which water is dealt with) that can be found in every country in the world appear as the combination of the various characteristics of the swimming human, the ball human, the track and field human, the dance human, and the martial arts human, and, although they are rarely seen in the swimming phenomenon, it is possible to see aspects of the skating human and the skiing human as well. Furthermore, the phenomena emphasize the becoming of a swimming human as these characteristics, and the phenomena are linked to these characteristics.

For example, things such as the record for the 100-meter crawl, the word "crawl," the phrase "100 meters," the sounds of the water and the sounds of the human that are heard during the 100-meter crawl, and the sounds made by those watching the event-all of these words, voices, and sounds are formed within the relationship of the human and the water in the swimming phenomenon. Thus, they all arise from the existence of the swimming human.

I have already presented, in the form of a hypothesis, the idea that the phenomenon of swimming is the mutual actions of the human and the water, which is therefore the phenomenon which promotes the swimming human and is the becoming of the swimming human.

However, in order to convert this to a thesis, I must plan to provide evidence for whether or not this is in fact the existential essence in the phenomenon of swimming. On the other hand, in order to make swimming a science, it is necessary to make clear the object of research for this field. In other words, I must confirm whether or not the phrase "swimming human" provides the realistic nature of the phenomenon of swimming.

I believe that I will be able to proceed with this method in the form of the Ontology of the Swimming Human. Specifically, using the term "swimming human," I will explain the factual existence of swimming (the phenomenon of swimming which occurs in every country in the world). From this evidence (this is a philosophical method, so I use the term "evidence"–in the case of the scientific method we say ''proof') the fact that the swimming human is the existential essence of the swimming phenomenon and the fact that the swimming human should be the object of scientific research in swimming will become clear. Then, it will be possible to go on from the ontology to develop a teleology and a methodology. Thus, the theory of swimming will be formed. When swimming studies are broken down from the "everyday-ness" of general human life into special areas and these areas are given names, the special field of swimming studies will be formed.

I have grasped the existence of the swimming human as three aspects, and, using them, I will attempt to explain this existence. These aspects are the social existence of the swimming human, the educational existence of the swimming human, and the movement-cultural existence of the swimming human. The swimming human exists in every country in the world in many different ways, pointing to the fact that it forms a special world. I begin my task with this understanding of the existence of this swimming human.

3

The Movement-Cultural Ontology
of the Swimming Human

Movement-culture is ingrained in the swimming human, and the swimming human exists possessing movement-cultural aspects. This comes from a connotative structure and a denotative structure. Together they maintain independent functions while living and existing as a whole.

THE CONNOTATIVE STRUCTURE

The swimming human as a movement human is organically composed with a head, torso, hands, and feet. Internally, he is composed of muscles, bones, organs, a brain, etc., that all rely on blood for their actions. Meanwhile, the swimming human as the movement of the water appears in many different aspects. For instance, he can appear as the movements of fresh water, salt water, sea water, river water, pool water, cold water, hot water, etc. Thus, there are many different water movements that are considered those of the "conscious" water, which acts in the swimming human in order to let the swimming human swim. If we classify these into large groups, we can separate them into man-made water and natural water. All of these act based on the natural actions of gravity, temperature, weather, air pressure, sunlight, etc., and man-made actions, such as an indoor pool, lighting, etc. Both as the behavior of an individual or as the behavior of a group, these actions act as the actions of skill. However, these actions all act in combination with the actions of perception, thought, and emotion that are based on the living body of the swimming human as a movement human. Therefore, the swimming human as a movement human appears as the synthesis of many different actions.

In the actions as an individual, both the swimming human as a movement human and the swimming human as the water movement sides mutually approach, contact and separate. These actions are composed of the actions of striking, kicking, grasping, pulling, inserting, stroking, diving, etc. Actually, based on these actions, the words *strike, kick, grasp, pull, insert, stroke, dive,* etc., have been created. Also, based on these actions, various sounds are also formed.

In the actions as a group, both the swimming human group as a movement human and the swimming human group as a water movement sides display the aspects of mutual approach, contact, and separation. These actions of the group are composed of the actions of yelling, signs, gestures, etc. Also, within the actions of the two sides of the swimming human group, various sounds are formed.

Furthermore, the actions of skill of both the individual and the group are based on the actions of the eyes, nose, tongue, ears, skin, etc., of the swimming human as a movement human, the actions of its internal organs such as the stomach, the heart, and the lungs, the actions of all types of bones, the actions of the cerebrum, the mid-brain, and the cerebellum, etc. In other words, the skilled actions rely on the actions of external sensations such as sight, hearing, taste, touch, and smell, and the internal sensations from the organs, bones, muscles, brain, etc. In addition, the actions of thought and emotion also contribute.

In other words, while this "sensation/thought/emotion" system's parts have independent functions, they are organically and dynamically related and participate in the skilled actions of the swimming human as a movement human. In making value judgments about skilled actions, such as good/bad, achieved/not achieved, the swimming human as a movement human relies greatly on the actions of this "sensation/thought/emotion" system. For example, decisions and conflicts such as "my head hurts/keep playing hard," "tired/time to quit," "I swallowed water/it's salty," "I'm losing/feels awful," "the teacher's watching/try my best," etc., point to the dynamic actions of "sensation/thought/emotion," "sensation/emotion," "sensation/thought," "thought/sensation," "emotion/sensation," "emotion/thought/sensation," and so on.

THE DENOTATIVE STRUCTURE

The swimming human as a movement human appears in various movement-cultural aspects. If we were to classify these movement-cultural aspects, we could classify them into the following four types.

The first type of swimming human is the swimming human in the phenomenon of swimming in which the individual human separates from the water (which is actually unthinkable in reality) or in which the individual human acts in a manner as to approach the water. The diving human is an example of this first type.

The second type of swimming human in the phenomenon of swimming is that in which the water and the individual human mutually approach each other and separate from each other. The crawl human, the breaststroke human, the backstroke human and the butterfly human are examples of this second type.

While the above types one and two possess movement-cultural characteristics of the individual, the following types three and four possess movement-cultural characteristics of the group.

The third type of swimming human in the phenomenon of swimming is that in which the actions of the group swimming human as a movement human attempt to approach the water or separate from the water. The diving human of a group is one example of this type.

The fourth type of swimming human in the phenomenon of swimming is the swimming human in which the group swimming human as a movement human and the swimming human as water movement repeat actions of mutual approach, separation, and contact. The 200-medley relay human, the group synchronized swimming human, and the group canoe human are examples of this fourth type.

In this manner, it is possible to classify the movement-cultural existence of every swimming phenomenon based on the substance and type of the actions of its swimming human (refer to Figure 21). However, each swimming human as a movement human exists in a manner that presents unique aspects. The crawl human exists with unique aspects not found in the breaststroke human. The diving human exists with unique aspects not found in the crawl human. The synchronized swimming human exists with unique aspects not found in the breaststroke human. Therefore, each type of swimming human appears in its own unique movement-cultural aspects.

DIVING-NESS (THE DIVING HUMAN)

The swimming human as a movement human exists in aspects of diving. For example, there is either a direct or indirect relation to the equipment of diving, the rules of diving, the facilities of diving, the terminology of diving, etc. The appearance of the diving human as a movement human forms the unique world of diving.

CRAWL-NESS (THE CRAWL HUMAN)

The swimming human as a movement human exists in aspects of the crawl. For example, there is either a direct or indirect relation to the equipment of the crawl, the clothing of the crawl, the rules of the crawl, the facilities of crawl, the terminology of the crawl, etc. The appearance of the diving human as a movement human forms a unique world of the crawl.

CANOEING-NESS (THE CANOEING HUMAN)

The swimming human as a movement human exists in aspects of canoeing. For example, there is either a direct or indirect relation to the equipment of canoeing, the clothes of canoeing, the rules of canoeing, the facilities of canoeing, the terminology of canoeing, etc. The appearance of the canoeing human as a movement human forms the unique world of canoeing.

SYNCHRONIZED SWIIMMING-NESS
(THE SYNCHRONIZED SWIMMING HUMAN)

The swimming human as a movement human exists in aspects of synchronized swimming. For example, there is either a direct or indirect relation to the equipment of synchronized swimming, the clothes of synchronized swimming, the rules of synchronized swimming, the facilities of synchronized swimming, the terminology of synchronized swimming, etc. The appearance of the synchronized

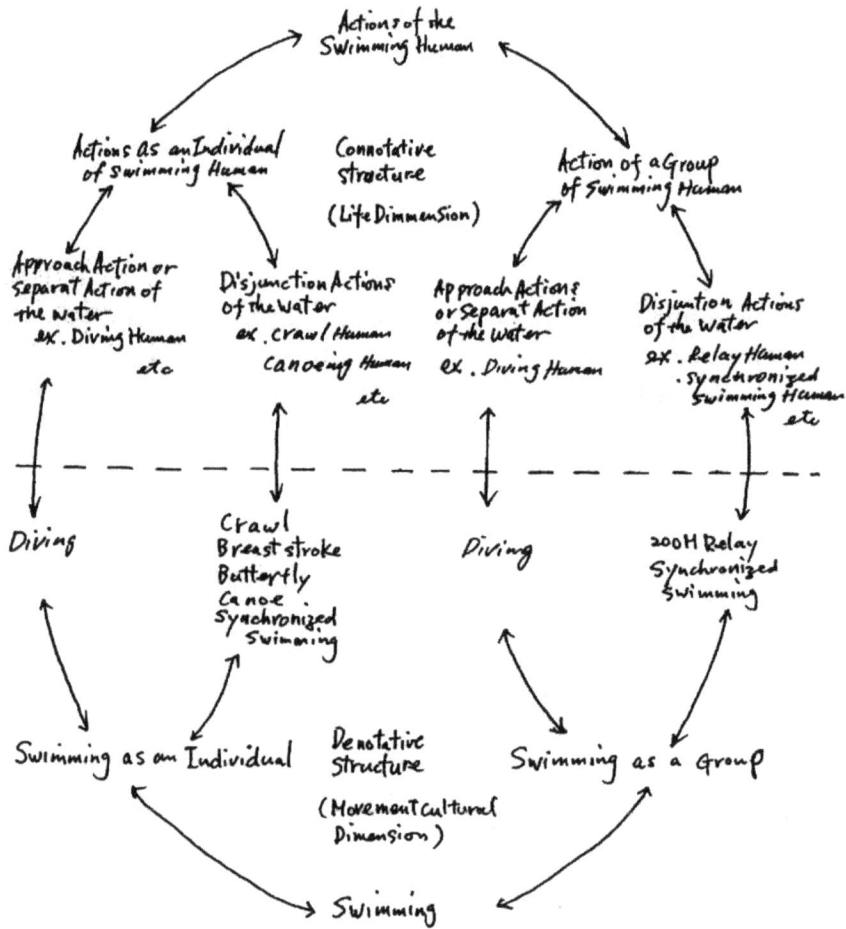

Figure 21. The Movement-Cultural Existence of the Swimming Human

swimming human as a movement human forms the unique world of synchronized swimming.

RELAY-NESS (THE RELAY HUMAN)

The swimming human as a movement human exists in aspects of the relay. For example, there is either a direct or indirect relation to the equipment of the relay, the clothes of the relay, the rules of the relay, the facilities of the relay, the terminology of the relay, etc. The appearance of the relay human as a movement human forms the unique world of the relay.

YACHTING-NESS (THE YACHTING HUMAN)

The swimming human as a movement human exists in aspects of yachting. For example, there is either a direct or indirect relation to the equipment of yachting, the clothes of yachting, the rules of yachting, the facilities of yachting, the terminology of yachting, etc. The appearance of the yachting human as a movement human forms the unique world of yachting.

Furthermore, it is possible that the types of special human existence connected with the swimming human will increase in the future. This is because the sports scientists of the world are always encouraging the development of new swimming events through creativity and new devices. I believe that, when this occurs, we must recognize and accept these new swimming events.

In this way, the swimming human as a movement human appears in many different movement-cultural aspects and exists in every country in the world, in every town, and even in schools. The swimming human appears in these many different movement-cultural aspects in America as Americans, in the Soviet Union as Soviets, and in Japan as Japanese.

4

The Educational Ontology of the Swimming Human

In the special society of physical education in every country in the world, the swimming human as a movement human exists possessing a "physical education human" side. Every type of swimming is evaluated educationally. Certainly, opinions are formed about whether a swimming builds strength, develops character, fosters mental growth, fosters creativity, etc. The educational existence of the swimming human as a movement human comes from a connotative structure and a denotative structure. Each works based on an independent structure, and as a whole they educationally exist.

THE CONNOTATIVE STRUCTURE

In order to make clear the actions of the swimming human, we will analyze them and use integrated judgment, by both looking from the actions of the swimming human toward the living energy and from the living energy toward the actions of the swimming human. In this manner, we can fully grasp the entire substance of the actions of the swimming human. We have some factors which are expressed, such as body, physical condition, body strength, flexibility, etc., while in contrast, some factors are expressive, such as the mind, soul, character, personality, condition of character, morale, flexibility, etc. These factors work in a living, separate manner, and the actions of the swimming human are the integration of all of these living elements. By using these words to inquire about the nature of the actions of the swimming human, we can elucidate the concept of the swimming human. Therefore, these words refer to the various partial factors that make up the swimming human, and they are living words. The source of these words is based upon the supply and demand of living energy produced by the unification (digestion, oxidation) that takes place inside the individual of the mutually conflicting elements of air, food, and the existence of the swimming human. In other words, the source is the transformation of the various elements, such as body, body strength, flexibility, physique, physical condition, mind, soul, morale, flexibility, personality, condition of character, etc. into a living entity. Therefore, the words body, body strength, flexibility, physique, physical condition, mind, soul, morale, flexibility, personality, and condition of character are all living words, and are words that have come to refer to reality.

On the other hand, we have said that the action of the swimming human is formed from a synthesis of the various types of actions of the swimming human expressed as mind, body, soul, physique, physical condition, body strength, flexibility, personality, condition of character, morale and flexibility, yet it should be noted that in our analysis of the actions of the swimming human we said that there is both a water movement and a movement human side to the swimming human, with mutually different objects. Since this is the case, it may not be appropriate to use the same type of language to explain both. However, based on the common point of view that both share as the swimming human, I will use the same language to explain them.

The analysis and synthesis of these two sides, the swimming human as a movement human and the swimming human as a water movement, are described by Figures 22 and 23.

Figure 22. The Types and Content of the Actions of the Swimming Human

I.   The visible physique of the swimming human
   • Water's size, temperature, etc.
   • Human's body weight, height, arm extension, height when sitting etc.
II.   The condition of the visible physique of the swimming human
   • Quality of the water, salt content, buoyancy, etc.
   • Condition of the human body, quality of organs

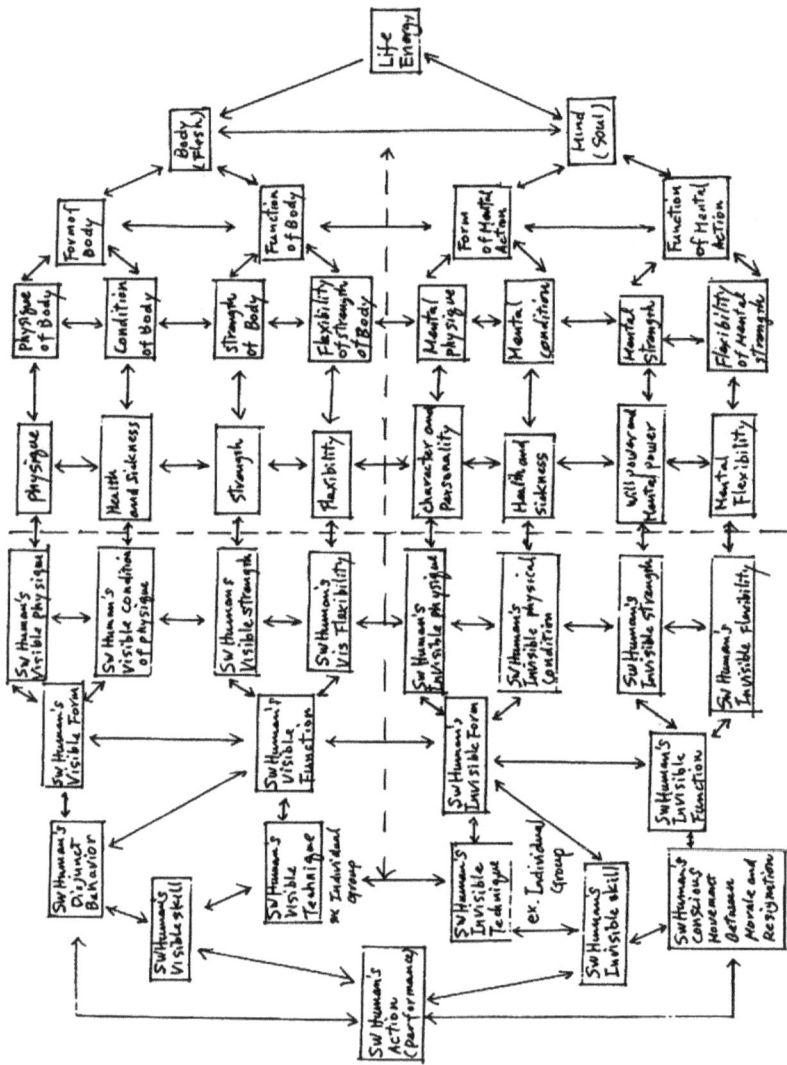

Figure 23. (Swimming Human Skilled Action Types) ←→ (Swimming Human Life Energy Types)

III. The visible physical strength of the swimming human
- Endurability and speed ability of the water–time strength
- Endurability and speed ability of the water–space strength
- Endurability and speed ability of the human–time strength
- Endurability and speed ability of the human–space strength

IV. The visible flexibility of the swimming human
- The effective physical ability and flexibility of the water
- The effective physical ability and flexibility of the human

----

V. The invisible physique of the swimming human
- Introversion and extroversion of the water
- Introversion and extroversion of the human

VI. The condition of the invisible physique of the swimming human
- Quality of the character of the water
- Quality of the character of the human

VII. The invisible physical strength of the swimming human
- Endurability and speedability of the morale of the water–time strength
- Endurability and speedability of the morale of the water–space strength
- Endurability and speedability of the morale of the human–time strength
- Endurability and speedability of the morale of the human–space strength

VIII. The invisible flexibility of the swimming human
- The flexibility of the morale of the water
- The flexibility of the morale of the human

Also making up the actions of the swimming human are skilled actions, which express technique. However, if we analyze these skilled actions, we can see that they are made up of actions of the conduct of the swimming human and the substance of the kind of technique being expressed. In other words, the actions of the conduct of the swimming human, together with the substance of the technique, make up the reality of the skilled actions of the swimming human and exist united in reality. These exist in a relationship that is mutually life-giving and enlivened, creating the phenomenon of the skilled existence of the swimming human.

THE DENOTATIVE STRUCTURE

In regard to the denotative structure of the educational existence of the swimming human. I have attempted some analytical speculation which will explain it as shown in Figure 24.

Figure 24. The Educational Existence of the Swimming Human

	First Analysis	Second Analysis
Educational phenomenon of the swimming human	Entire Expression of swimming human (social standpoint)	Sociality (objective) Discovery-ness (subjective)
	Partial expression of swimming human (Individual standpoint)	Cooperativeness (objective) Creativity (subjective)

Here, I will explain each of the educational elements of the swimming human dealt with in the second analysis of the educational phenomenon of the swimming human.

Sociality

The swimming human functions in the special society of swimming. However, in order to create this special society, it must work by accepting and approving all of the factors. Specifically, the swimming human as a movement human that takes on the special social role of "player" acts both socially and morally. The swimming human as a movement human acts in participation with the humans that take on the social roles of judges, teachers, leaders, etc., and even with things that are set up for the purpose of becoming a swimming human as a movement human, such as unique facilities, equipment, rules, etc. In this manner, the phenomenon of swimming is when, as the swimming human as a movement human is enlarged from some person to some thing and from some thing to some person, it acts both socially and morally. However, while the sociality of the swimming human as a movement human provides the nature of a special sociality, in order that swimming occurs in general society, it exists in the twofold relationship with general society and the special society of swimming.

DISCOVERY-NESS

The swimming human as a movement human acts creatively. At the same time, the swimming human as a water movement also acts creatively. In the actions of the swimming human, there are situations in which new technical content or form, of which no similar example existed in the past, are added. These new techniques are conceptualized and given special names. This itself points to the discovery-ness of the swimming human. For example, names such as *flip turn, rotating dive,* etc., point to the discovery-ness of the swimming human. Also, in the future, the improvement of techniques or the introduction of some new element into the swimming phenomenon may create a new existence of the swimming human and form a new movement-cultural history. All of these are the discovery-ness of the swimming human, which comes forth from the experience of becoming a swimming human. The discovery-ness of the swimming human consists of both the creative and historical development aspects of these actions.

COOPERATIVENESS

In the phenomenon of swimming and the phenomena in which water is dealt with, there are many cases in which the swimming human acts in a group. In these cases, cooperative intentions are demanded of the swimming human. This cooperativeness is a social action that depends on the mutual relationship between acting swimming humans that have taken on the special roles of swimming. In the cooperativeness of the swimming human, there is cooperativeness from a unified standpoint, and cooperativeness from a different standpoint. For example, the general factors associated with the individual swimming human such as the school, the region, age, sex, etc., may be identical or different. Also, the various factors from the special standpoint of swimming such as skill level of the swimming human, the role of "competitor," companions, etc., may be identical or different.

In this way, the actions of the cooperativeness of the swimming human exist as the nature of the identities and differences of general things and the identities and differences of the special things limited only to swimming. So if we try to limit it to only the cooperativeness in the special society of swimming, the cooperativeness of both identity recognition of the swimming human and difference recognition of the swimming human is based on the recognition of the existential standpoint.

Creativity

The swimming human, in the living, always-changing space of swimming, is at every moment faced with the problem, "In what way should I best handle the water?" The swimming human as a water movement, which has been acted on by the swimming human as a movement human, is a concrete expression of the skill of the swimming human as a movement human itself. It is something that indicates the level of the skill. Therefore, the swimming human as a water movement demands skill from the swimming human as a movement human, and, conversely, the swimming human as a movement human exists while demanding skill from the swimming human as a water movement. Through the skill demands of these two sides, the swimming human creates. For example, the water which acts in combination with the diving human as a movement human to perform the social role of "diving" (or, the swimming human) acts as the skill of the diving human as a movement human to perform the social role of "diving." The diving human that stands facing the water attempts to, using perceptions, skillfully adjust the individual's body appropriately. As a result, actions such as the quality of the revolutions, success or failure, etc. will be decided.

The creativity of the swimming human can be seen in the creativity of the partial cause/effect actions of diving and entering, kicking and being propelled, touching and being touched. Through this partial cause/effect process, the action of winning, the action of losing, and the action of a draw are created. Creativity can be seen in the partial cause/effect actions in the entire process of swimming, from start to finish. Furthermore, the creativity generates the subjective emotions of happiness, vexation, anger, and sorrow at every instant in the swimming human as a movement human. In this manner, the swimming human as a movement human and the swimming human as a water movement, in the special living space of swimming, the unknown space of swimming, and the regulated space of swimming, are acting creatively in an original way. These actions bring about a reformation of the self-consciousness of the possibilities of ability in the swimming human which has taken the special social role of "competitor" or "swimmer." In this special society, it gives meaning to life.

In this way, the swimming human exists educationally. At the same time, it exists as the educational beings in scholastic physical education in every country in the world, and is an expression of every country in the world in its existence.

5

The Social Ontology of the Swimming Human

The swimming human exists within general society. There it exists while possessing an aspect of social existence in which it lives trying to plan original plans. For example, from the factual phenomenon of swimming, all kinds of words have been derived, such as "to do sports," "to do physical education," "to do recreation," etc. On the other hand, in the social actions of the swimming human, there are various kinds of social language that have been created, such as "fair," "unfair," "cooperative," etc. This can be said to be implicit proof that the swimming human exists socially. Concerning the social existence of the swimming human, in order to grasp its factual living state as a living state, I will divide this into a connotative structure and a denotative structure and explain each. Therefore, the social existence of the swimming human is the entirety of the independent actions of connotative structure and denotative structure.

THE CONNOTATIVE STRUCTURE

Let us consider the basic aspects of the actions of the swimming human. In the case of the individual, it is the actions of mutual separation/contact within the swimming human (between the human and the water). In the case of the group, it is the actions of mutual separation/contact between many swimming humans. In other words, the basic principle is the entirety of the motion that occurs when the swimming human as a water movement and the swimming human as a movement human mutually separate, approach, and contact.

If we apply this fact to each kind of the entire phenomenon of swimming, it will be easily understood. This is described by Figure 25.

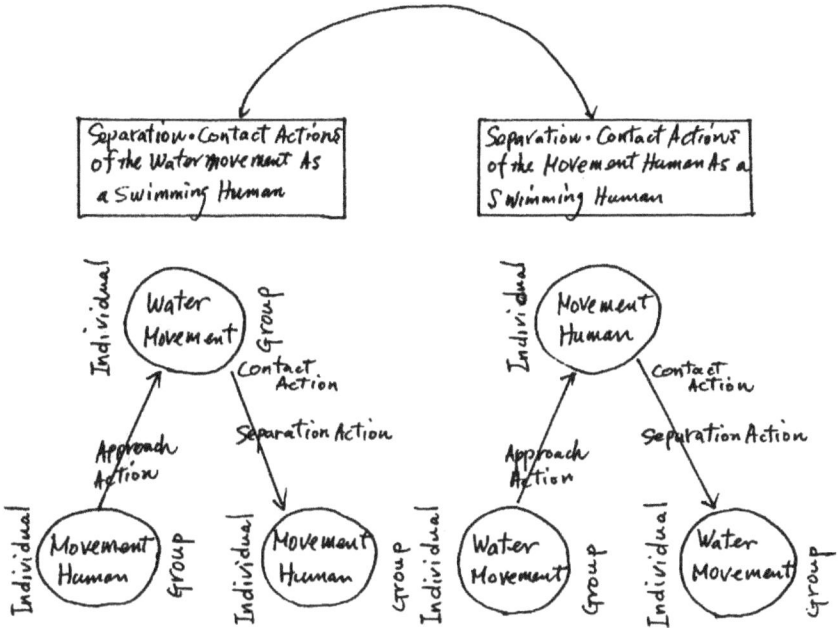

Figure 25. The Separation/Contact Actions of the Swimming Human

In other words, in order to grasp this dynamic separation/contact relationship within the swimming human, one must begin by looking objectively from the actions of the body of the swimming human. Meanwhile, there are also the actions of the mind of the swimming human, namely the separation/contact movement of consciousness. Those actions come from the fact that when dealing with the water, the swimming human as a movement human recognizes the water by the action of unconscious-conscious. The strength, or perhaps weakness, of the actions of the consciousness of the swimming human as a movement human is located in the polarized structure of the morale and resignation of the consciousness. The strength or weakness depends throughout on the manner in which the consciousness moves between this polarization.

As the swimming human as a movement human lives, breathes, and goes to the swimming human as a water movement, and as the swimming human as a water movement lives, breathes, and goes to the swimming human as a movement human, the morale strengthens the consciousness. In other words, the morale strengthens the unified perception of both sides of the swimming human, the swimming human as a movement human and the swimming human as a water movement, as a swimming human. It also promotes the manifestation of living as a swimming human. For example, in a hotly contested free-style competition, the water seems to be an extension of the competing swimming human's (movement human's) body, and various shouting is generated, such as "He won!" or "He lost!" In addition, voiceless thoughts are also created.

Because the morale of the swimming human is a living thing, it promotes flattering aspects, but since it is caused through the consciousness's condition of resignation, it moves to the resignation, which is a different kind of element. Primarily, the morale of the swimming human is in the dimension of time, which has a passive nature and has some bad points, but in the dimension of space, it has an active nature. The morale possesses these kinds of properties.

However, the resignation of the swimming human is the condition of the consciousness of the preparation steps for displaying the consciousness of morale. Therefore, the resignation of the swimming human, in relation to the morale, is an element of denial, but on the other hand, it provides a kind of quality that serves to support morale as well. In the realm of space, the resignation of the swimming human is weak and passive, but in the realm of time it is strong and active.

The connotative structure of the social existence of the swimming human presents the mutual actions of separation-contact within the swimming human. Objectively, the body acts by the separation-contact actions, and at the same time, subjectively, the mind acts by the separation-contact actions. Together they act as a whole. Within these actions, the changes in consciousness are acting; namely by presenting the aspects of morale and resignation.

Concerning the actions of the swimming human, we use many different expressions to express them. These different expressions all rely on the aspects of the actions of the swimming human. (Refer to Figure 26.)

Figure 26. Natural Expressions Related to the Actions of the Swimming Human

Names of Actions of the Swimming Human as Water Movement:	Names of Actions of the Swimming Human as Movement Human:
splashing	hitting
foaming	striking
being entered	kicking
being dived into	inserting
being kicked	diving
being stroked	touching
etc.	stroking
	etc.

For example, in order to make sentences for classifications within the types of swimming humans, such as for the actions of the crawl human, the diving human and the breaststroke human, one would proceed in the following way:

The crawl human as a movement human acts by kicking the water and stroking the water with the hands. On the other hand, the crawl human as a water movement acts by splashing and foaming when being kicked and stroked by the hands.

The diving human as a movement human acts by diving in 1the water, while the diving human as a water movement acts by being dived into and splashing.

In the preceding manner, the actions of the connotative 1 structure of the swimming human themselves act in an original way. At the same time, they also act with aspects of denotative structure.

THE DENOTATIVE STRUCTURE

In the following way, I have analyzed and gained insight into the denotative elements of the social existence of the swimming human, and I have attempted to extract the denotative elements themselves. (See Figure 27.)

Figure 27. The Social Existence of the Swimming Human

	First Analysis	Second Analysis
The Aspects of the Social Existence of the Swimming Human	Entire Expression of the Swimming Human	Recreation-ness Competitiveness Sports-ness Physical Ed.-ness
	Partial Expression of the Swimming Human	Combativeness Cooperativeness Primitiveness Modernity

From the preceding chart, I will explain each of the social factors of the swimming human listed in the second analysis.

Recreation-ness and Competitiveness

First there is recreation-ness, in which the swimming human amuses itself with swimming, such as when using company free time with a group of co-workers or during a family get-together. There is also competitiveness, which includes the tension of seriousness, such as when competitive leagues are commissioned by the sponsorship of competitive groups. The recreation-ness of the swimming human fosters a place for the meeting of the hearts of the swimming human as a movement human comrade and the swimming human as a movement human and the swimming human as a water movement comrade. It is a softening aspect that encourages mutual understanding. Then there is competitiveness, which is the aspect of the swimming human where, within the rules of competition, a swimming human as a movement human comrade, or perhaps a swimming human as a movement human and a swimming human as a water movement comrade facing one another, act with bravery and valorous determination. The greater the scale of the competitive league, the more the spirit intensifies, and the competitiveness of the swimming human appears more conspicuously. For instance, this is the case in all the types of swimming in the Olympics and all types of swimming in inter- national leagues, etc.

Physical Education-ness–Sports-ness

In the phenomenon of swimming, based on the fundamental structure of the teacher and pupil, the educational environment and content are given in the school's pool or corresponding place. This is the physical education-ness of the swimming human doing swimming. The physical education-ness of the swimming human is an educational phenomenon which depends on the sum total of the teacher and pupil. This is an aspect of the swimming human that can come from the special society of the school, a narrowly defined area. The student, who is recognized by the school side, perhaps specially selected, from nursery school through elementary, junior high, and high school, will be acting the role of the physical education-ness of the swimming human. On the other hand, the phenomenon of swimming in general society is an expression of the sports-ness of the swimming human. The sports-ness of the swimming human is the aspect of the swimming human in which, in the social phenomenon that relies on the sum total of leaders and followers, a wide range of many kinds of games are developed with no relevance to sex, age, or occupation. For example, there are swimming tournaments sponsored by local, national, and international groups. These are appearances of the sports-ness of the swimming human.

Combativeness-Cooperativeness

In the actions of the swimming human, there are the contrasting actions of combativeness and cooperativeness. The action of swimming of an individual swimming human as a movement human on a team of swimming humans is an expression of cooperativeness. This action stroke and kick among companion swimming humans creates a oneness of the team/individual, and builds many conscious states. It conspicuously expresses the cooperativeness of the swimming human. This aspect can also be seen in the phenomenon where a group does swimming, where as actions of the swimming human, the skilled actions of the swimming human as an individual are sublimated to the skilled actions of the swimming human as a group. Thus, when there is a lack in the skilled actions of one individual swimming human as a movement human, it is compensated for by the skilled actions of some other individual swimming human as a movement human. In addition, there is also the aspect in which in order for one swimming human as a movement human as an individual to do skilled actions, some different swimming human as a movement human as an individual tries to give assistance. In these forms, this aspect appears.

In contrast to this, there are also times when, with a stern attitude towards other swimming humans, the swimming human as an individual attacks the swimming humans that are enemies. This is an expression of the combativeness of the swimming human. It is most conspicuous in the setting of vehement competition between swimming humans. Combativeness can be seen in every phenomenon of swimming and every phenomenon in which water is dealt with. It is the moment when the skilled actions of the swimming human as an individual are steeply opposed to the skilled actions of some other swimming human as an individual and they attack each other. It also can be the moment of attack that appears between the skilled actions of swimming humans of a group.

Primitiveness-Modernity

In swimming or in any phenomenon in which water is dealt with, there is the primitiveness of the swimming human, in which the swimming human engages in direct body contact. Of course, swimming humans normally wear bathing suits, which differ based on sex and individual taste, but the portions of the bodies outside the bathing suit often come into contact. These aspects are the primitiveness of the swimming human. Also, the ancient Greek swimming humans used to appear as swimming humans that were completely naked. This, too, is probably a typical aspect of the primitiveness of the swimming human. In addition, the direct stroking and kicking of water is a primitive part of the swimming human.

Therefore, the primitiveness of the swimming human imparts a direct jolt to the body of the swimming human as a movement human, and the handling of the water is relatively possible.

On the other hand, there is an aspect of modernity of the swimming human, in which in the relation between swimming humans, the swimming human acts by using equipment. For example, in a canoe or a boat, the actions between the water and the human in the phenomenon of swimming are indirect. A paddle or body weight is used to act out these actions. Recently, swimmers wear glasses, put on caps, or wear fashionable bathing suits. None of these promote direct contact with the water. Instead, these are expressions of the modernity of the swimming human, which encourages an indirect relation between the water and the human.

Moreover, there are various things that regulate the social existence of the swimming human. For example, the amateur-ness or professional-ness of the swimming human, the fitness of the swimming human, the fair play-ness of the swimming human, and the playfulness of the swimming human, are vital elements that act to support the social aspects of the swimming human. In this manner, in every country in the world, the swimming human expresses the originality of each country and carries on a social existence. In the stream of time of past- present-future, this existence lives in the present as realistic beings, and this existence is variable and alive.

6

Generalizations from the Ontology of the Swimming Human

Up to this point, the three existences of the swimming human, namely the educational, social, and sports-cultural existences, have been clearly explained. The words *swimming human*, when taken as in the hypothesis, are part of language that refers to the existential essence of the phenomenon of swimming and the phenomena in which water is dealt with. In other words, we have confirmed the fact that the words *swimming human* are alive and exist, forming the special expanding world of swimming and dealing with water in every country in the world. We have also confirmed the fact that these words refer directly to a special kind of human. The swimming human exists as the expression of each country in the world, in America as Americans, in the Soviet Union as Soviets, in China as Chinese, in Japan as Japanese, and in Sweden as Swedish. In the present of the ever-flowing stream of past-present-future, with living and variable aspects, it exists and lives.

Now, as a result of the clear evidence of the existential essence of swimming and the clear evidence of the existence of the swimming human in the phenomenon of swimming, the following kinds of questions can now be answered:

Question 1: What is the phenomenon of swimming?
Answer: This is the phenomenon in which, when a human and water perform swimming, they do not become a human and water, but instead both sides become a swimming human.

Question 2: What does it mean to do swimming?
Answer: This is when some humans become swimming humans that can be divided into, on the one hand, a movement human and on the other hand, a movement water.

Example:
Question #1: What does it mean to do the crawl?
Answer: This is when a human and water become a crawl human
Question #2: What does it mean to do the breaststroke?
Answer: This is when a human and water become a breast stroke human.

Question 3: What does it mean to do swimming in physical education?
Answer: This is the conduct in which the human becomes a swimming human as a movement human and a swimming human as a water movement, and both of these are physical education-ized and try to become physical education-ized.

Question 4: What does it mean to do swimming in sports?
Answer: This is the conduct in which the human becomes a swimming human as a movement human and a swimming human as a water movement, and both of these are sports-ized and try to become sports-ized.

Question 5: What does it mean to do swimming in the Olympics?
Answer: This is the conduct in which the human becomes a swimming human as a movement human and a swimming human as a water movement, and both of these are Olympic-ized and try to become Olympic-ized.

Question 6: What does it mean to do swimming in recreation?
Answer: This is the conduct in which the human becomes a swimming human as a movement human and a swimming human as a water movement, and both of these are recreation-ized and try to become recreation-ized.

Furthermore, this swimming human encompasses every type of swimming human. Namely, it is the existence of the crawl human, the existence of the diving human, the existence of the breaststroke human, the existence of the backstroke

human, the existence of the synchronized swimming human, etc. Also, depending on the differences in sex, age, race, school, occupation, etc., the above exist as different expressions. Differences in countries and regions also result in different expressions.

In the above manner, through the movement of speculation, the establishment of the ontology of the swimming human, from both an abstract standpoint and a concrete standpoint, from the existence to being, and from being to existence, became possible. Here, we can generalize this system as the ontology of the swimming human.

Finally, while I have referred to the existence of the swimming human as a special existence of the human in swimming, I must now go on to present the existence of a purpose in the existence of the swimming human. This is because, today, all types of swimming are being practiced in physical education programs. Also, this necessity comes from the practice of sports in every country in the world. This practice should be autonomous and recognized as a path toward righteousness. Thus, I would like to confirm the swimming human image, which comes from the existence of the swimming human, which exists with special aspects in swimming.

7

The Teleology of the Swimming Human

Until this point, I have contemplated the existential essence in the phenomenon of all types of swimming, namely the existence of all types of the swimming human. I have clearly shown and confirmed that in every country in the world, every type of swimming human exists in the world of each type of swimming. However, at the same time, this existence includes the purpose of the swimming human, namely the swimming human image. It is not simply the existence of the swimming human, but also an existence that tries to realize the ideal image that the swimming human must attain. Above all, the practice of all types of swimming that is being conducted in scholastic physical education in every country in the world is being practiced for the sake of the realization of all types of the swimming human image by all types of the swimming human. Also, there is the necessity for physical education and sports studies research concerning all types of swimming in every country in the world (such as physical education and sports studies philosophy, physical education and sports studies psychology, physical education and sports studies physiology, physical education and sports studies sociology, physical education and sports studies history, etc.) in order to plan the realization of the swimming human image, in the practice of swimming or the practice where water is dealt with, in physical education.

At this point I will go on to speculate about what kind of special ideal image is meant by the purpose of the swimming human, or more specifically, by the swimming human image.

The swimming human image is, of course, the purpose of the practice of the swimming, but it is necessary to clearly explain to what in reality it is which this word directly refers. It refers to the ideal image in which the actions of the swimming human as a movement human and the actions of the swimming human as a water movement in the practice of swimming are existing together doing superior actions. The a swimming human image is the ideal image that is living and I exists ideally from one era to the next in every country in the world. This is determined by the research of the physical education and sports theory specialists (such as physical education and sports studies philosophers, physical education and sports studies psychologists, physical education and sports studies physiologists, physical education and sports studies sociologists, physical education and sports studies historians, etc.) that are living in each era in every country in the world. The words swimming human image are referring directly to the ideal existence which adds weight, depth, size, and breadth to that acting existence.

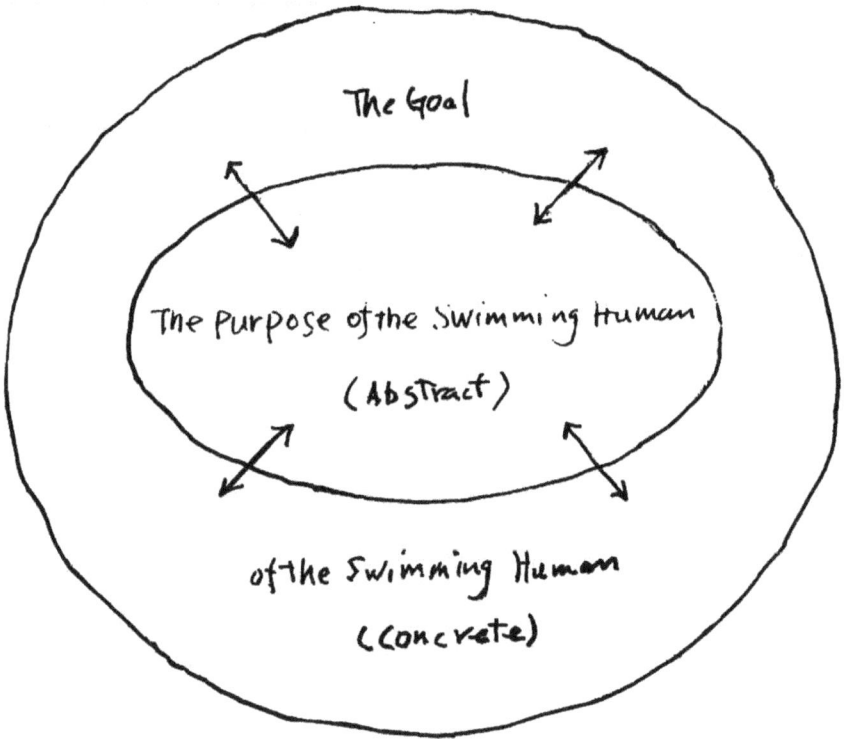

The Goal

The Purpose of the Swimming Human

(Abstract)

of the Swimming Human

(Concrete)

Figure 28. Constitution of the Swimming Human Image

In the nature of the substance of the swimming human, there are really two different kinds of natures. Also, these two natures dynamically act together and form the firm swimming human image.

The first is the part of the purpose that has a universal nature that is common, no matter what the time, no matter what the place, no matter what the country. For example, all of the superior actions of the movement human and the water movement, in other words the attempt to realize the swimming human image, even though there are differences between the histories, cultures, ideas, race, etc., of all the countries in the world, share a common universal nature.

The second is the concrete purpose of the swimming human, which is variable depending on the time, the society, age, sex, and other things that are different from country to country. In every country, there is originality in history, ideas, and culture. The swimming human image of a certain era in each country of the world has the aspects of that era. Furthermore, from the point of view of age, the various types of the swimming human image for children are different from the various types of the swimming human image for old people. From the point of view of sex, the swimming human image for males and females is different. The image of the swimming human is not identical, due to the various ways of differing. Therefore, as opposed to the purpose of the universal substance of the swimming human, this points to the variable, concrete purpose of the swimming human. The constitution of the teleology of the swimming human relies on the support/being-supported relationship between these two sides, which is a relationship that acts dynamically and mutually to support each side. The swimming human image of the former is the *purpose* of the swimming human, while the swimming human image of the latter is the *goal* of the swimming human. The difference between these words clearly points to the difference between the universal purpose and the variable purpose. Therefore, the swimming human image consists of the purpose substance as its core, and that which surrounds the purpose substance is the goal substance. The dynamic relationship between them assumes the character of abstract/concrete-concrete/abstract. Because of this, the swimming human image possesses unifying qualities that transcend the realities of time, nationality, age, sex, etc., but at the same time, this teleology is also one that sees those realities as realities. This can be summarized in Figure 28 (previous page).

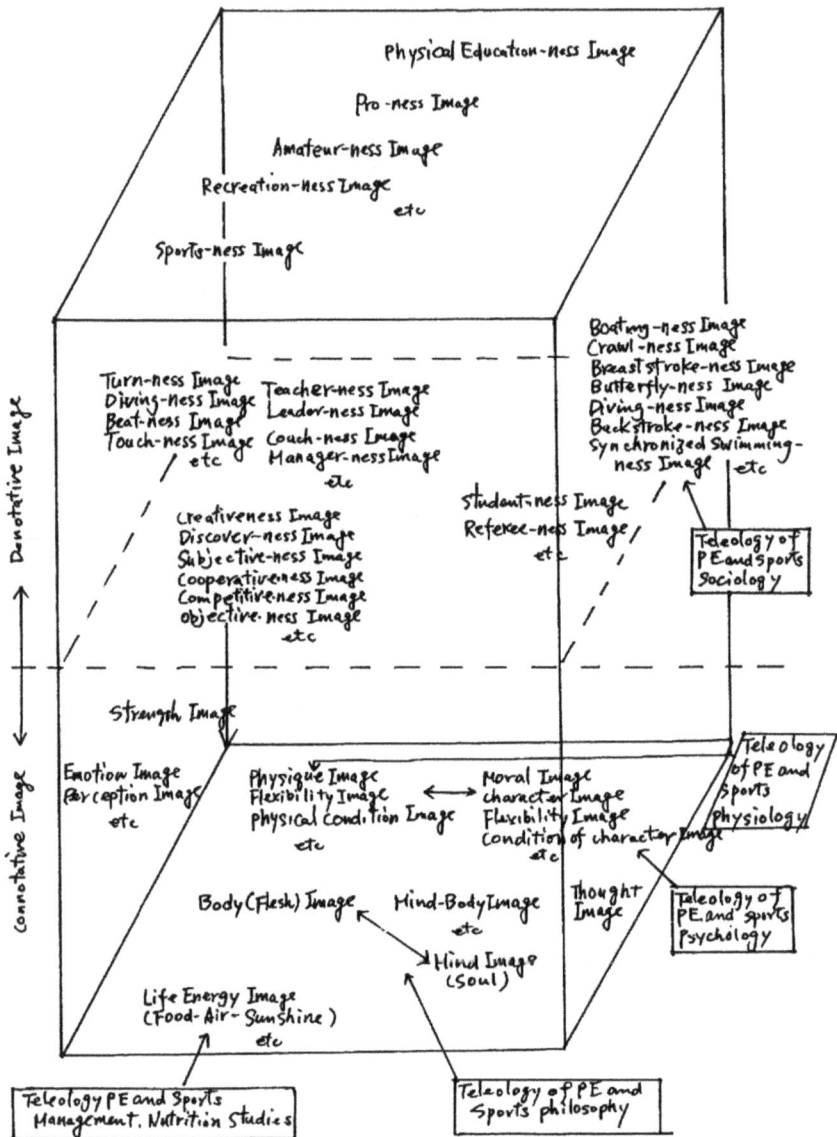

Figure 29. The Swimming Human Image*

*In physical education and sports, the swimming human forms the special society of the swimming. It works ideally in a unique way. At the same time, it is regulated in a unique way and exists ideally.

Next, I would like to go on to explain the purpose of the swimming human. Specifically, of what substance is the swimming human image itself constructed? I will now explain this point.

The structure of the swimming human image is made up of two types of structure: a connotative structure and a denotative structure. These form the living, unified whole. There are the actions of all of the many element images, and as a whole they act ideally. If we broadly divide these various idealistic elements, they come from the connotative structure and the denotative structure (refer to Figure 29).

THE IMAGE OF CONNOTATIVE STRUCTURE

In the actions of the swimming human image, there is the image of connotative structure. This acts as the foundation of the generation of the image of denotative structure, and so this is a vitally important area. The image of connotative structure itself is formed from the various element images that become the many different ideals. It is formed from the ideal of the image of life energy that comes from physical education and sports nutrition studies and physical education and sports hygiene, the ideal of the image of the body and the image of the mind (mind-body image) that come from physical education j and sports philosophy, the ideal of the image of body strength, the image of flexibility, the image of physique and the image of physical condition (the image of health) that come from physical education and sports physiology, etc. The physical education and sports studies researchers of every country in the world will go on to prove the realistic existence of the swimming human. Relying on the leadership of this proof, the previous images of the connotative structure of the swimming human will be concretely alive and acting ideal images. Then, in order that the physical education and sports studies researchers of every country in the world expand on the substance of the words of these various elements, and in order to promote understanding of these words as living things, the research of purpose will proceed. As a result, to the question "Why are the educational ministries of every country in the world conducting and practicing all kinds of swimming in scholastic physical education?" one will be able to provide a direct answer from the various fields of physical education and sports studies, namely physical education and sports philosophy, physical education and sports psychology, physical education and sports physiology, physical education and sports sociology, physical education and sports history, etc. For example, from physical education and sports philosophy, all types of swimming are practiced in scholastic physical education in order to realize the image of the mind and body of all types of the swimming human image. The content of the image of the mind and body can be explained relying on the research of physical education and sports philosophers. Of the content of the partial element images presented here, all are ideal content that are drawn from the proof of the all of the specialist researchers in physical education and sports studies. And at the same time, in the space of the various elements in the image of connotative structure, they are things that are doing superior actions.

Also, these are the various elements that do superior actions in the image of the denotative structure as well. For example, "the image of body strength" is the superior inner actions of body strength itself, acting in superior actions in relation to the various elements, such as morale, flexibility, cooperativeness, competitiveness, physical condition, creativeness, etc.

As is shown above, the image of the connotative structure in the swimming human image is the entirety of the various elements of the connotative structure that have been amassed by the physical education and sports studies researchers in every country in the world and the physical education and sports studies research of every era. However, this image of connotative structure acts not only in the image of connotative structure, but is also an image of connotative structure that works in the image of denotative structure. So, what kind of substance of ideal images makes up the image of the denotative structure of the swimming human? I will now go on to deal with this question.

THE IMAGE OF DENOTATIVE STRUCTURE

In the actions of the swimming human image as a swimming human image, there is an image of denotative structure. In the ideal image that is generated from the image of connotative structure, the origin of the formation of the image of the denotative structure is included. Inside the denotative structure itself, which acts as the denotative structure, are the actions of the various element images.

Looking from the specialized point of view of the physical education and sports sociologists and scholastic physical education, and considering the existential direction of the swimming human, if an inquiry is made to determine the ideal images of that existence, then in the following way, the idealistic elements of the denotative structure become visible. The image of sports-ness, the image of physical education-ness, the image of amateur-ness, the image of professional-ness, the image of trim-ness, the image of recreation-ness, the image of teacher-ness, the image of student-ness, the image of leader-ness, the image of follower-ness, the image of coach-ness, the image of crawl-ness, the image of backstroke-ness, the image of butterfly-ness, the image of synchronized swimming-ness, the image of diving-ness, the image of yachting-ness, the image of canoeing-ness, the image of baseball-ness, the image of first swimmer-ness, the image of creativeness, the image of cooperativeness, the image of competitive-ness, the image of objectiveness, the image of discovery-ness, the image of subjectiveness, etc. From the above kinds of images of elements, the image of the denotative structure in the swimming human image is formed. The above various images of elements are the various aspects of the swimming human image, and they are things that have been culled from researchers in physical education and sports sociology and scholastic physical education. Then, the images of the various elements in the denotative structure act in a way that promotes the idealistic condition of the connotative structure, while at the same time they are the superior denotative elements that act in a way that promotes the idealistic condition of the elements in the image of the denotative structure. Therefore, each of the elements in the denotative structure themselves are elements that are superior and act ideally.

In the above manner, the swimming human image itself is the purpose of the existence of the swimming human in every country in the world. Therefore, this is limited by the existence of the swimming human, and in reality there is a purpose in straining to derive the swimming human image from this existence. For example, in order to explain this swimming human image as a swimming human image in reality, we can divide the swimming human image into its various different types, such as the crawl human image, the diving human image, the breaststroke human image, the synchronized swimming human image, and so on. We can concretely express the goal of the swimming human if we look, for instance, at the breaststroke human from various points of view. From the point of view of school level, there are the elementary school breaststroke human image and the college breaststroke human image. From the point of view of sex, there are the male breaststroke human image and the female breast-stroke human image. From the point-of-view of age, there are the ten-year-old breaststroke human image and the forty-year-old breaststroke human image. From the point of view of nationality, there are the breaststroke human image as an American, the breaststroke human image as a Japanese, the breaststroke human image as a Soviet, the breaststroke human image as a Swede, the breaststroke human image as an Australian, and so on. In other words, because the existence of all types of the swimming human in every country of the world is different, the purpose of the swimming human can be materialized as different goals. On the other hand, while the swimming human image can make as its purpose the various unique swimming human images of each country in the world, from a global, humanistic, common point of view, it can also present a purpose that is the swimming human image as a world citizen. The image of swimming human provided that the existence of all types of the swimming human practicing all kinds of swimming in all places around the world can be confirmed, this purpose can be erected as a common purpose of all types of the world citizen (or perhaps mankind) swimming human image.

Above, I have presented the purpose of the swimming human, or more specifically, the substance of the swimming human image (limited to only the important substance necessary in swimming theory). As a result, we have reached a point owing kinds of questions can be answered:

Question 1: Why are the educational ministries of every the world practicing all types of swimming in physical education?

Answer: All types of swimming are being practiced in on in every country in the world in order to realize all types of the swimming human image as the peoples of every country in the world.

Question 2: Why are the educational ministries of every country in the world doing classes on the theory concerning all types of swimming in scholastic education?
Answer: This is so that in the scholastic education of every country in the world, physical education teachers will show the peaceful practice of all types of swimming to the students, and so that they will explain the practice of all types of swimming to the students and the students will understand them.

Question3: Why is the IOC doing all types of swimming in the Olympics?
Answer: The IOC is practicing all types of swimming so that, in the Olympics, all types of the swimming human image will be realized.

Question 4: Why are the physical education and sports researchers of every country in the world conducting research in fields such as physical education and sports psychology, physical education and sports philosophy, physical education and sports physiology, physical education and sports history, physical education and sports sociology, etc.? Furthermore, is it necessary that they do so?
Answer: This is so that in the place of swimming in every country in the world, the swimming human image of every country in the world will be realized. This research is the guarantee of the peaceful practice of swimming in every country. Also, in order to answer the question "Why must the educational ministries of every country in the world, the IOC, and sports groups be made to recognize and practice all types of swimming?" directly from theory, this is necessary and important research. Relying on the execution of this research, the practice of swimming will be guaranteed to be a peaceful practice.

Question 5: Why must a World Physical Education and Sports Academy be established?

Answer: Relying on the development of this type of research, the swimming human image in every country in the world and the swimming human image of each age of mankind will be constructed, thus developing the guarantee of peace in every country and world peace. Also, the academy will nurture physical education and sports researchers who will contribute to peace in every country and to world peace.

Question 6: Why must a Physical Education and Sports Academy be established in every country in the world?

Answer: Physical education and sports researchers (from every field) are necessary to construct swimming theory in every country and to guarantee that the practice of swimming in every country in the world is a peaceful practice. They will promote research with meaning that contributes to peace in their countries. At the same time, it is also necessary to nurture national doctorates in every country, and to nurture physical education and sports researchers who will contribute to world peace through swimming studies research in every country.

In addition, any questions concerning the purpose of formation related to all types of swimming in every country in the world can be answered from the Teleology of the Swimming Human. Also, through the purpose, it is necessary to go on to develop support for peace in every country and world peace.

Furthermore, from the presentations of the Ontology and Teleology of the Swimming Human in every country in the world, we must now go on to develop the Methodology of the Swimming Human in every country in the world by which the existence of the swimming human in every country in the world realizes the swimming human image of every country in the world. This will deal with the method by which the existence of the swimming human in every country in the world realizes the swimming human image. The Methodology will be organically connected to the Ontology and the Teleology, and will have the unique quality that it will work together with them. This kind of undertaking will work through the realization of the establishment of universal swimming theory, which unites all countries in the world and accepts differences between all countries in the world.

8

The Methodology of the Swimming Human

The Methodology of the Swimming Human is an original theoretical area that deals with both the movement human and the water movement sides of the phenomenon of all types of swimming. These two sides, which are referred to directly by the term "swimming human," can be said to be able to, depending on how they work together to emphasize an intent on harmony, realize the swimming human image. For example, if we emphasize the water movement, only the ability required for the water movement is required of the movement human. On the other hand, if we emphasize the movement human, only the ability required for the movement human is required of the water movement. Therefore, achieving the required ability that is possible when both sides accept each other's demands is imperative. This type of method is the only advanced method by which the swimming human image can be realized. Toward that end, there are notably two methodologies: one in relation to time, and one in relation to space. The former considers the experience of becoming a swimming human in terms of time, while the latter considers the experience of becoming a swimming human in terms of space. Therefore, the method that realizes the swimming human image must give the appropriate weight to experience in time and experience in space.

THE THEORETICAL FOUNDATION AND GROUNDS FOR THE FORMATION OF THE SWIMMING HUMAN METHODOLOGY

Before presenting the Methodology of the Swimming Human, it is necessary to first make clear the reasons why it is possible to present such a methodology. In order to do this, we must look at the theoretical foundation and the grounds for the methodology. The theoretical foundation for the formation of the Methodology of the

157

Swimming Human relies on the Educational, Social, and Movement-Cultural Ontologies of the Swimming Human and the Teleology of the Swimming Human already presented. The grounds for the formation of this methodology is the fact that in scholastic physical education in every country around the world swimming is being practiced. The former is based on the development of the theory, while the latter comes from the practice of swimming.

THE CHARACTER OF THE METHODOLOGY OF THE SWIMMING HUMAN

There are two characters associated with the content of the Methodology of the Swimming Human. First, it is an unchangeable, universal, abstract methodology, applicable to any country at any time. Second, as countries and times change, it is a concrete, realistic methodology that changes accordingly. The Methodology of the Swimming Human is constructed with the former at the core, while the latter surrounds it, both working together to preserve the relationship. More specifically, the former is the area of the methodology based on the common qualities of all countries and constructed by the physical education and sports researchers of every country in the world so that the practice of swimming in scholastic physical education in every country in the world serves to realize the swimming human image. Meanwhile, the latter is the area of the methodology that has the quality that it grasps the differences in the realistic aspects of the swimming human, i.e. country, time, age, sex, school, etc., as differences in realistic aspects.

ELEMENTS OF THE FORMATION OF THE CONTENTS OF THE METHODOLOGY OF THE SWIMMING HUMAN

In regard to the formation of the Methodology of the Swimming Human, both the theoretical foundation and the practical grounds have already been presented. However, I believe that the latter, the practical grounds, gives an extraordinarily important reason for the formation of the Methodology of the Swimming Human. Namely, because of the existence of the practice of swimming in physical education programs, the existence of the practice of swimming in society, and because of the existence of physical education teachers, mentors, pupils and students who play a function in society, the need for the Methodology of the Swimming Human becomes apparent.

In that case, physical education teachers and mentors are those who lead students to become swimming humans and realize the swimming human image, while students and followers who receive all forms of swimming education are those who look toward becoming all forms of swimming humans and realizing all forms of the swimming human image. Therefore, the human relationships of the teachers and mentors and students and followers in the phenomenon of swimming will all become the swimming human and realize the swimming human image. It is a mutual relationship that exists to realize the swimming human image.

Those fostering the swimming human have experience in the past of fully becoming a swimming human in order to realize the swimming human image. They are those who possess the leadership qualifications to be able to realize the swimming human image. On the other hand, those becoming swimming humans must receive leadership in order to realize the swimming human image. They are those of whom study ability is demanded.

With the relationship between physical education teachers, who try to realize the swimming human image and foster swimming humans, and students, who study while looking toward becoming swimming humans and realizing the swimming human image, as the grounds, the various structural elements of the methodology of the various kinds of swimming humans are formed. Specifically, these elements include study, leadership, evaluation, curriculum, educational resources, study ability, study processes, leadership ability, skill, etc. Classifying these elements into large groups, we may divide them into study, leadership, and educational resources. The terms "skill," "study ability," study processes," etc., are all terms connected with the student or follower becoming a swimming human and trying to realize the swimming human image, and are therefore "study" terms. The terms "leadership ability," "evaluation," "curriculum," etc., are all terms connected with the teachers and mentors trying to realize the swimming human image and turn their students into swimming humans, and are therefore "leadership" terms. Finally, that which brings the leadership and study together at the place of swimming are the educational resources. The structural elements of the Methodology of the Swimming Human are systematized in the manner described in Figure 30.

Figure 30. The Structural Elements of the Methodology of the Swimming Human

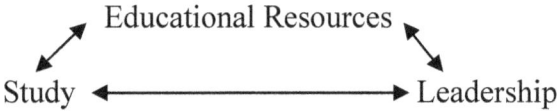

Educational Resources

Study ←——————————→ Leadership

Study. This is the state of those becoming swimming humans in which they learn all of the various things they must learn from those helping them to become swimming humans in order to realize the swimming human image. Also, we will call "students" those who, under the supervision of those fostering the swimming human, strive to learn that which they need to become a swimming human. Furthermore, "study ability" is ability that students possess to learn all the constructive knowledge required in order to become a swimming human and realize the swimming human image. "Skill" is a part of study ability, and is the condition of the mastery of the necessary techniques required to become a swimming human and realize the swimming human image. Also, "study process" is the process by which, under the leadership of those fostering the swimming human, those becoming swimming humans learn all of the relevant knowledge.

Leadership. This is defined as the leading of those who will become swimming humans by those who will foster their becoming swimming humans by giving them all the various knowledge they will need toward the goal of realizing the swimming human image. "Leadership ability" is the ability of those fostering swimming humans, with the goal of realizing the swimming human image, to fully develop those becoming swimming humans. The "leadership process" is the process by which those fostering swimming humans, with the goal of realizing the swimming human image, lead those becoming swimming humans. Furthermore, "evaluation" is the process by which those fostering swimming humans decide what level those becoming swimming humans have reached and how far they have advanced in approaching the realization of the swimming human image. "Curriculum" is the study route through which those fostering swimming humans lead those becoming swimming humans in order to realize the swimming human image.

Educational Resources. We collectively use this term to refer to all materials those fostering swimming humans use to lead those becoming swimming humans to realize the swimming human image along with all study materials used by those becoming swimming humans aiming to realize the swimming human image. Therefore, the educational resources play the role of intermediary in the formation of the leadership and study of the swimming human, and are a necessary methodological element in the realization of the swimming human image. The educational resources include natural educational resources and man-made educational resources. The former are sunshine, air, weather (clear, rain, snow, clouds), air pressure (wind), water (water in a pool), surfaces (river bank, sea bottom), etc. The latter include a natorium, heater, pool, mats, ball, yacht, boat, canoe, kayak, etc. Therefore, in the broad sense of the word, "educational resources" refers to the combination of natural educational resources and man-made natural resources, but when taken in the narrow sense of the word, refers mostly to man-made educational resources.

THE CONSTRUCTION METHOD OF THE
METHODOLOGY OF THE SWIMMING HUMAN

It is imperative that we use the terminology of the structural elements of the Methodology of the Swimming Human, namely study (skill, study process, etc.), leadership (evaluation, curriculum, leadership process, leadership ability, etc.) and educational resources in order to realize the swimming human image. However, it is also

161

necessary to answer the question of how the content of these elements can be given substance. I will now present these kinds of problems related to the construction of the Methodology of the Swimming Human.

From the standpoint of those dealing with fundamental theory of physical education studies, it is possible to construct a methodology that answers these kinds of questions. The Methodology of the Swimming Human should use the original specialized vocabulary from each specialized area of physical education, and considering study, leadership, and educational resources, etc., we can create a separate methodology from each field of physical education that serves to realize every partial image of the swimming human that emerges from that field. In regard to the Methodology of the Swimming Human from physical education physiology, for instance, while considering study, leadership, and educational resources, we can construct an original methodology, using the specialized terms of physiology, such as strength, physique, health, and flexibility, that serve to realize the strength image, the physique image, the health image, and the flexibility image of the swimming human.

Likewise, in regard to the Methodology of the Swimming Human from physical education psychology, while considering study, leadership, and educational resources, we can construct an original methodology, using the specialized terms of psychology, such as character, morale, health, flexibility, etc., that serves to realize the character image, the morale image, the health image, and the flexibility image of the swimming human. In regard to the Methodology of the Swimming Human from physical education philosophy, while considering study, leadership, and educational resources, we can construct an original methodology, using the specialized terms of philosophy, such as mind, body, the mind-body relationship, soul, flesh, etc., that serves to realize the mind image, the body image, the mind-body image, the soul image, and the flesh image of the swimming human. In regard to the Methodology of the Swimming Human from physical education educational science, while considering study, leadership, and educational resources, we can construct an original methodology, using the specialized terms of educational science, such as creativity, subjectivity, objectivity, cooperation, competition, etc., that serves to realize the creativity image, the subjectivity image, the objectivity image, the cooperation image, and the competition image of the swimming human. In regard to the Methodology of the Swimming Human from physical education sociology, while considering study, leadership, and educational resources, we can construct an original methodology, using the specialized terms of sociology, such as starter, fourth lap swimmer, second finisher, fourth finisher, amateur, recreation, etc., that serve to realize the starter image, the fourth lap swimmer image, the second finisher image, the fourth finisher image, the amateur image, and the recreation image of the swimming human. In regard to the Methodology of the Swimming Human from biomechanics, while considering study, leadership, and educational resources, we can construct an original methodology, using the specialized terms of biomechanics, such as kicking, striking, stretching, grasping, etc., that serves to realize the kicking image, the striking image, the stretching image, and the grasping image of the swimming human. Moreover, the construction of the original methodologies of the swimming human for each of these specialized fields of physical education must be living, changing entities, taking into account the realistic existence of things such as nationality, race, age, sex, etc., to always be the best methodology for physical education researchers of the present time. Therefore, research specialists in each field of physical education must, while referring to the knowledge in physical education history for advice, construct separate methodologies responsible for each specialized field.

In the above manner, it is possible to construct a Methodology of the Swimming Human for every country in the world.

9

The Path Toward an Olympics in Which the Physical Education and Sports Studies Researchers of Each Country in the World Compete

CONCLUSION

Up to this point, the hypothesis has been presented, extracting the existential essence from the phenomenon of swimming. In order to prove the hypothesis, the ontology was presented based on philosophical methods. In philosophical terms, this is clear evidence. In addition, from the ontology, the theory was developed further in both the teleology and the methodology, thereby furthering progress up the steps of formation of Swimming Theory (world unified and different). With Swimming Theory, which is simply a collective term for the theories concerning every type of swimming, we can go on to further the formation of scholarship in areas such as breaststroke studies, crawl studies, backstroke studies, canoe studies, diving studies, etc. In other words, this is a scholarship of practice (a theory) dealing with practice. This will be formed as theories of each type of swimming study dealing with the practice of each type of swimming.

This Swimming Theory will appear as the fundamental theory for the purpose of constructing swimming studies in every country in the world. More specifically, it will be a theoretical system for constructing physical education and sports studies in every country in the world. With regard to the differences of history, thought, culture, etc., that exist between countries, this will be a theory that will be applicable to every country in which all types of swimming are practiced in physical education and in society. In addition, it will also be applicable to the practice of swimming in the Olympics held by the IOC. This Swimming Theory will deal with the whole theories of swimming studies, while also dealing with the partial theories from every field of physical education and sports studies, namely physical education and sports philosophy, physical education and sports psychology, physical education and sports physiology, physical education and sports sociology, etc. While consulting the facts in physical education and sports history and using the specialized terminology of every field, it will elucidate the realistic phenomenon of each type of swimming through experiments, surveys, and data. It will be able to confirm the scholarship as necessary to unify, from each specialized field, the ontologies, teleologies, and methodologies of all types of swimming humans in every country in the world, in every era. At the same time, these partial theories will fit into the entire theory, namely Swimming Theory, and promote the establishment of scholarship in crawl studies, breaststroke studies, diving studies, canoe studies, etc. With the completion of this theory, the question "Why are all types of swimming being conducted by the educational ministries in scholastic physical education in every country in the world?" will be answered to general society from the standpoint of physical education and sports researchers. This means that the theory will carry a social responsibility to the practice of swimming in every country. Also, the theory will be able to answer the question Why are social sports groups in every country and international sports groups (i.e., the IOC's Olympics) conducting all types of swimming?" from the standpoint of the world's physical education and sports researchers. Therefore, the various specialized research in physical education and sports studies based on the Swimming Theory will be important social and nationalistic research that will have impact on the peaceful unification of differences between all nations. Thus, to those who achieve success with partial theories, it will be possible to award a physical education and sports studies doctorate (national doctorate) degree. Furthermore, the grounds and theoretical basis for the worthiness of these partial theories of the doctorate degree can be explained to general society and guaranteed through the Swimming Theory. In other words, the doctorate degree in physical education and sports studies will gain social and international trust when evaluated as being objectively responsible, both within the country and without. The physical education and sports studies doctorate, which can be explained by the Swimming Theory, will be registered with the education ministry in each country as a mark of achievement of physical education and sports research.

The standards and principles of this Swimming Theory must be defended to the slightest degree by physical education and sports researchers of the world in order to preserve the health of physical education and sports studies in every country in the world. If the countries of the world, or even some country, tries to conduct research concerning swimming without paying attention to this Swimming Theory, several severe problems will result, including tasteless and dry research that is void of knowledge and isolated from the phenomenon of swimming, a lack of connection between the physical education and sports researcher and his nation and society, and chaos stemming from confusion of knowledge. Thus, physical education and sports research will surely fall into the trap of conducting physical education and sports research for the sake of spending (wasting) money. Therefore, we must fairly evaluate whether or not countries are applying this Swimming Theory and whether or not they are conducting true physical education and sports research. Above all, in order to conduct physical education and sports research, we must recognize physical education and sports theory as necessary, and from its principles develop research. Without physical education and sports theory, there can be no physical education and sports research.

In presenting this Swimming Theory to the physical education and sports researchers of every country in the world, I hope to insure a common object of research for the physical education and sports researchers in each country. I would like to make sure that each researcher is self-conscious in advancing research. In addition, I hope to demonstrate the social responsibility of physical education and sports researchers. In performing this role, I am contributing to society and to physical education. Also, this effort will lead us to the path to world peace and peace in every country, and with this presentation the first step has been taken towards this development. When the physical education and sports researchers in every country in the world awaken national consciousness and world consciousness, social unity, national unity, and even world unity will be born. Eventually, this theory, as a theory of the Olympics that deals with the practice of the Olympics, will lead to progress in the direction of the establishment of a World

Physical Education and Sports Academy (ICHPERSD in USA). At the same time, we must promise that physical education and sports studies will not be governed by other areas of scholarship, but will crystallize as an independent study on their own.

Bibliography

Edmund, Fusserl. *Ideen* 1. N.P.: Verlag Von Max Niemeyer, 1922.

Hegel, Georg Wilhelm Friedrich. *Samtliche Werke 4; Wissenshaft der Logik Zweiter Teil (The Research for Logic in the Second Volume)* N.p.: George Lasson, 1923.

Hideo, Kondo. *Taiku no Tetsugaku (The Philosophy of Physical Education).* Tokyo: Reimei Press, 1951.

Kitaro, Nishida. *Zen no Kenkyu (Research on Virtue).* Tokyo: Iwanami Press, 1966.

Lindsay, A. D. *The Philosophy of Bergson.* N.p.: J. M. Dentsons Ltd., 1911.

Nishida, Kitaro. *Tetugaku Rombun shu (Collection of Philosophical Essays)* Vol. I, 7. Tokyo: Iwanami Press, 1945.

Kuki, Shuzo. *Iki no Kozo (The Structure of the Beauty of Consciousness).* Tokyo: Iwanami Press, 1974.

Earle F., Zeiglar. *Sport and Physical Education Philosophy.* Camel Benchmark Press, 1989.

www.ingramcontent.com/pod-product-compliance
Lightning Source LLC
Chambersburg PA
CBHW031844090426
42741CB00005B/342